The Prodigal Woman

The Prodigal Woman

Lee Hayes

VISION HOUSE PUBLISHERS

Santa Ana, California 92705

PREFACE

This book is not intended to be a literary work of art. On my own, I have nothing clever or astounding to say, just a desire to tell a real story.

The story is true, and has been written to possibly share something of value with that man or woman who walks the same meaningless gangplank that I once walked. I want to let you know that there is an answer to your dilemma. In a world that tells you, "Be free; do your own thing," you yet live in conflict as you are left to wonder, "What am I all about? Who am I important to? Where is the love I need so badly?"

This book is for the young woman who has begun to feel more like a slave in a "free society" and cannot relate to the liberated woman. It is also for the young man who fights his desire to run from the pressures of "responsibility" and feels he can't measure up to today's image of success.

I dedicate *The Prodigal Woman* to that human being who has begun to feel cheated and left out somewhere along the way. I want to let you know that there is a love that never fails.

Lee

I

FROM BEHIND THE steel-barred window of a smelly, dirty Mexican jail, I watched helplessly as my two little girls, ages two and four, were being led away in the custody of a tall American woman whom I knew to be a marijuana pusher. Their tender voices rang back, "Why does mommy have to stay in that place?"

Through the window I watched the hot noonday sun work to peel away more paint from the small run-down stucco buildings which lined the dry dirt roads. Curious onlookers mingled just outside my cell. Two people moved and blocked my view of the girls as they walked across the road. "Please, please!" I yelled. "Get out of the way." And my voice trailed to a sob.

Alesen and Lauri strained to turn and see me as I cried out, "No — no — no . . . bring them back. Don't take them away from me." I wept.

Then the woman clutched the girls' hands, rounded the corner, and the three figures were out of sight.

Stunned and motionless, I hung onto the bars that kept me from freedom, aware only that the air was thick and stale in that tiny enclosure. The reality of

7

the outside world crept out of reach, and suddenly I was terribly alone. Overpowering fear and hate welled up from the very center of my being.

Gasping for air, I turned and slid slowly down the wall. Finding myself in the corner of the floor, the air I breathed was heavy with urine and human filth. I buried my head in my arms and pounded on the floor with my fists, screaming to some distant God who just had to be bigger and more loving than any human being I had ever known.

My soul fragmented as I recalled that just moments before my husband, Phil, had turned me over to the Mexican police. He called me a lunatic. All my identification and legal papers were taken from me. My children were ripped out of my arms, and I watched them disappear, not knowing if I would ever see them again.

Hysterical with fear and anger, I was dragged off through the jail door, and like an animal I was locked behind a heavy steel gate. Local Mexican residents and tourists alike had gathered to watch this wild display of inhumanity, and I could turn to no one. Now here I sat — twenty-six years of life hopelessly crashing to a tragic end, the conclusion of a trip originally designed to provide all the romance and excitement a young family could yearn for in a lifetime.

Just barely conscious that I was even a human being, I lay on the floor of that cell still pounding softly, mechanically, with my fists. Where is that God of love my mother used to tell me about? I asked myself. With defiance I recalled how she had said that God was in the trees, the sky, and the ocean. Well, where was a tree now? I could see no blue sky here. There was no ocean in that cell to give me solace.

The hatred inside distorted any memory of beauty. What could I cling to? "Where are you, God?" I cried out loud.

I have no idea what took place, but four hours later someone pulled my body off the floor as if lifting a heavy wet blanket. I heard Phil's voice in conversation with a Mexican official.

"It's your personal beezness," he told Phil. "Take your wife and work theese out yourself."

I was pronounced "free to go" and the authorities washed their hands of the whole affair.

Freedom from jail only meant bondage to a man I no longer knew — a man who raged at the sight of me and spewed hatred with every breath. Phil and I walked out of the building together, but he kept five or six paces ahead, looking back only to order me to keep up.

The late afternoon sun gouged at my sore and swollen eyes. My face felt as if all the tears had raked my cheeks raw. With great effort I put one limp leg before the other as we walked through the little town.

It must have been *siesta* time, for as we walked, I noticed very few people in the streets and most of the shops were closed. I was relieved, for I was not anxious to have curious groups of people pointing

9

from a distance as they recognized the American lady whom they had seen earlier screaming in the streets and being thrown into jail.

Several long blocks later I caught up with Phil as he stood to unlock the door of a strange little house that was temporarily ours. He led the way through the door. I peered around the room and listened sharply for the girls' voices. They were not there. Not wanting to appear too anxious or suspicious, I slowly climbed the stairs — maybe they were napping in the bedroom area. When I didn't see them, I stiffened and wanted to scream but stood perfectly still as I heard Phil walk up behind me.

Trembling from weakness and fear, I thought, "What is going to happen now?" If I had any strength left, it had to be reserved to find the girls. "Where are the kids?" I asked in a meek voice as I turned bravely to face Phil. "Please go get them for me."

I learned instantly never to make the slightest demand on Phil, for at those words he grabbed my arm and growled, "If I bring Lauri and Alesen to you, you're not to make one move to leave this country."

Realizing that he was in full command and mine was not to question him again, I mustered up the last ounce of humility left and spoke. "Phil, I just want the girls with me. We won't go anywhere."

I waited for him to say something. With words as harsh as his stare he exclaimed, "I know you won't!" He glared long into my face, and I wondered what he saw there. Then he turned and was gone. When I heard the front door close downstairs, I stepped out on the balcony just off the bedroom and watched Phil walk aimlessly down the street. He was on his way to get Lauri and Alesen. I knew that he would not allow harm to come to them, for as horrible as things were, I knew too that he loved them as much as he possibly could.

From the balcony, one could look out over the tile rooftops and see our anchored fifty-two-foot schooner rocking back and forth in the bay. In the eyes of anyone else it might have appeared a picture postcard kind of view. But I saw only the object of my husband's attention and affection and suddenly understood why boats are referred to as *she*. *She* had lured my husband from me, and I stared like a jealous wife. This beautiful boat had originally left the coast of California to bring my husband, our two small children, myself, and four others to this point on a journey around the world that was to last four years.

I once had a love for her too. I had worked hard to get her shaped up and ready for a long sail. I had counted it a privilege to spend time with her on weekends — cleaning, scraping, painting, varnishing, and rebuilding her tired hull. She was beautiful. But now she was my enemy, my competition, and Phil was caught to choose between us.

II

PHIL HAYES AND I grew up together near Los Angeles in an obscure little town called Wilmar. It was later renamed South San Gabriel so it could be placed on the city map.

When he was seventeen and I was only ten years old, Phil strolled by where my little pal and I played in a park across from my house. He was one of the "older boys" in the neighborhood who hung around with my big brother. But on this day I was drawn to pay closer attention to him. He made some silly remarks just to begin a conversation and then asked me, "When you grow up, will you marry me?" I giggled, and he smiled and shrugged his shoulders with a wait-and-see kind of attitude.

From that day on a new interest for him sparked inside me, and I began to take more notice of this very handsome guy with curly blond hair and beautiful hazel eyes. Phil was a happy-go-lucky young man with no apparent interest in any one thing. My curiosity about him made me hang around the house a lot when he came to see my brother. Instead of going out to play, I eavesdropped on their discussions only to listen to his side of the conversation. I thought his

13

opinions about life were marvelous. When I dared to sit in the same room just to watch him, I became his wide-eyed captive audience as he told wonderful stories of intrigue for what seemed like hours on end.

Phil was not big in stature, but I never saw him in a small frame. To me he was a wondrous giant of a man — strong, happy, a joyous person who often broke into contagious laughter. He rarely elaborated on the serious and personal side of his life; yet there was an aura of serious determination about everything he did. For years I called it *courage*. He was beautifully put together and became more appealing as I got older. If Phil had a low opinion of himself as a young man, I never detected it.

Other than his whimsical proposal of marriage to me, his best friend says Phil never expressed a profound interest in anything until he got a job with a small louvred-window company. His boss encouraged and motivated him to become a salesman. A few extra night-school courses and some measure of success in sales gave him confidence that only he knew was lacking.

As the years went by, he would remind me of his desire to have me for his bride. But as I grew up, my mother encouraged me: "Build some castles in the sky." "The world is all yours," she said, "and you can have anything you want if you want it badly enough."

And I did want something. I wanted desperately to find out what life was all about, and most of all I wanted to know if there was anybody out there who answered to the name of *God*. Marriage was definitely *not* on my list of things to do.

Many, many times as a child, I would find myself studying the huge ocean from a distance. Without warning or prompting from anyone, I became struck with awesome wonder: Why is all that water even out there? Who am I and what is my purpose in relation to that beautiful yet hazardous stretch of sea?

Once while staring at some small goldfish in a bowl atop our bookshelf, I asked my mother, "Why am I a human being instead of a goldfish?" I think she said something about my having ancestors a very long time ago who were indeed fish. And then I was only left to ask, "Oh! Am I supposed to be better off than they were?" My questions stemmed from pure innocence as I wondered.

Or I'd ask myself, Is there some final purpose for my being born a girl, specifically, the last of four children to a particular man and woman who were not happy to be together?

As time passed I had to find out who and why I was and where I belonged in this thing called life. My mother later decided this was a spark of some deep intellectual interest and headed me in the direction of higher education. I couldn't figure out the connection. I thought the questions were simple and asked myself, Are the answers just so complicated I'd have to go to school the rest of my life?

My parents were divorced when I was eight years old. I was too young to care whether or not this situation brought immediate happiness to them, but it surely didn't provide happiness for me. My dad's absence was more obvious to me than his presence had ever been. There were two older brothers and a sister, and mom somehow managed to keep us together even though she struggled with her own personal problems while raising four children alone. She dealt with them in the best way she knew how, and all I knew was that she was my wonderful mother.

My fondest secret wish, however, was that one day she would come home with my dad at her side and say, "Woops! We made a mistake! Your father is going to live with us again." That never happened, though, and it wasn't until years later that I could understand why. Whatever their hopes, dreams, and expectations were when they fell in love simply collapsed without the foundation of understanding each other's unique and wonderful personality.

Our family was the forerunner of people "doing their own thing." Our friends envied us. They thought ours was a great fun and exciting way to live. The beer and good times could always be found at our house. But all I wanted was my dad, and I thought the most wonderful thing in the entire world would be to sit around a roast beef dinner on a Sunday afternoon with the *whole* family. I could not understand the simple facts that: (1), we could not afford the roast beef dinner, and (2), my mother and father could not get along under the same roof.

Ours was the Party House. We had real clambakes at 2:00 in the morning upon our return from midnight clam-digging at the beach. My oldest brother was in the Merchant Marines by this time; so quite often we had the added attraction of whole cases of imported French wines, "fresh off the boat."

Mother worked in the record section of a large department store downtown. In those days, famous artists made personal appearances in big stores to help the sale of their latest release, and my mother knew all the jazz musicians in Los Angeles. They were often invited to top off a party with a jam session at our house. Our neighbors either had to join the party or exercise a very high level of tolerance. Sometimes they just gave up and called the cops to restore the neighborhood to its much needed rest.

More often than not I felt alienated from my brothers as they sat long afternoons drinking beer and discussing a good book or how to rebuild a '39 Ford engine. I felt helpless with my need to be a part of their interests; so I just listened in the background as discussions turned to rather heated and intellectual subjects. Being the youngest, I had little to say in such matters.

Often adults don't stop to realize that busy, playful children are constantly absorbing and forming deep philosophical ideas about life. Since I was regularly referred to as the spoiled kid in the family, I tried in my childish way to stay out of everyone's path so they wouldn't find reasons to call me spoiled.

Loving the outdoors, I spent most of my time there, even in the evenings. We had lots of fruit trees on our property, and every summer I eagerly anticipated the fruit season. My mother worked every spare minute in the garden, and the results of her labor were sensational. People driving down the street would stop their cars to enjoy the charm of my mother and/or her garden.

One Sunday morning found me on the front porch watching my mother as she dug around her hollyhocks. I was usually bored and restless on Sunday mornings until my best friend could get home from church. I had gone to church with my friend before and remember asking several people, "Why is that guy hanging on that cross?" I never got an answer. And then one day I came home to discover that my mother didn't want me to go to church any more. She said we could have church out under a tree. Then she said the first words that made me really aware of God: "I don't believe God wants us couped up inside a building on Sunday or any other day."

This particular Sunday I sat on the edge of the porch crushing some crisp dirt clods under my foot and yelled across the lawn, "Mom, who's God?" I waited.

"Oh," she said with a grunt as she pulled at some tough weeds. "He's a god of love." That's good. I needed to know that. Then she gave a final yank on some devil grass and came to sit beside me to continue to share her insights on the matter. "He's in the trees, flowers, sky, and the ocean," she told me.

I enjoyed those wonderful moments together with my mother so much. The morning sun was bright and warm, and I remember how fresh the air smelled as I listened intently to her voice. The words she spoke were lovely, and it didn't really matter that her answers didn't seem to satisfy my question. But she spoke with such authority that I thought I now knew as much about God as anyone ever needed to know about him, and whatever need there was to know more just simply went unfilled.

I was proud of the labels *liberal* and *broad-minded* that were given our family. Truth and intellectual endeavors were our highest aim, with a whole lot of humor for balance. I believed this was sufficient for my life too.

When my sister married and my brothers were on their own, mom and I bounced around northern and southern California by ourselves. As a young girl, I looked for that intangible love from any boy who would show a sign of interest. Dating, however, was often frustrating and mostly a bore, but the ache to be loved seemed to increase just the same.

I was in and out of a half-dozen schools between junior and senior high, but I finally graduated. After high school, I worked as a secretary, and two years later sought the glamorous job as stewardess with a leading airline. This life provided a mixture of fun and frustration but certainly nothing that gave any hint of purpose or fulfillment. I didn't care for the way most of the gals spent their layovers. Not that I was above their wild dating activities — in fact I found myself encouraging my flight buddies in their escapades and got a kick out of their stories. But their "guy in every port" routine just wasn't my bag.

Due to our varied schedules, my roommates and I were seldom home at the same time. Consequently, I spent a great deal of time by myself. Everywhere I flew was foreign and lonely to me. The work itself was hard and kept me plenty busy. One of my passengers hired me as a part-time photographer's model, and I welcomed this diversion to help keep my schedule full. Later I was offered a glittery full-time job in New York but could only see more loneliness in that kind of future.

Phil kept in touch. We corresponded daily and talked on the phone infrequently. One night he called long distance after I had just returned to my apartment following a particularly frustrating flight. He was still waiting for me to give in and marry him. He literally caught me in a weak moment. I said yes, and we set a wedding date. Flying wasn't giving me any insight to what life was all about, and the only other alternative seemed to be marriage. I joyfully quit flying and two weeks later headed for a Las Vegas wedding.

The so-called ceremony made me feel a little like we were being run through a sausage factory, but there were a few meaningful moments. Phil was the typical nervous groom, and I was nearly oblivious to everything. The chapel minister rattled off a bunch of words as a matter of routine. He spoke with his eyes

20

raised to the ceiling and looked rather bored. Suddenly I caught a phrase that pierced my soul like a sharp knife: ". . . 'til death do you part."

With those words I looked at Phil and thought to myself, "I don't know what I'm doing, but whatever it is, it's going to last a long time and I'm willing." Time stood still until I voiced two small words of commitment, "I do."

We weren't married two hours before a lady cornered me in the powder room of one of the casinos. She had overheard me speaking of my brand-new marriage. Appointing herself my personal marriage counselor, she sauntered over to give me some advice. With liquor breath and slurring words, she began to warn me about the dumb thing I had just done.

"Marriage is for the birds," she breathed. I felt sad for this woman who strained to look closely into my face to focus. "You're a very foolish girl," she finished while poking me on the shoulder. Then she wobbled to catch her balance and moved out of sight.

Walking back out to the casino to find Phil deeply involved in a game of blackjack, I thought maybe my alcoholic adviser was absolutely right. Nevertheless, we didn't stay in Vegas. We finished off our honeymoon in Arizona and then settled down in Phil's apartment near the town where we both grew up.

After three weeks of marriage, we really fell in love! I never dreamed it could be so wonderful, and I was sure that this was the meaning of life: love, home, family. Real fulfillment at last. Phil was a successful young salesman, so our life together was full of people and activities. We traveled often on weekends to ski or go boating on Phil's small power boat.

Phil became my god, and I felt he could do no wrong. In fact I had heard the story of how Jesus walked on water, and I was sure that if anyone else could ever do it again it was my husband. When asked, "Do you believe in God?" my answer was a quick and impudent, "Of course, I do. I sleep with him."

III

PHIL HAD A DREAM, and I guess it was that dream that brought the first shadow across our otherwise bright lives. His ambition led him into the construction business. When he received his builder's license, he wanted to work hard, make lots of money, save as much as possible, and buy a sailboat big enough to make a round-the-world voyage.

At first I was excited about this plan. I wanted to do anything as long as it was with him. I looked up to Phil as though he were ten feet tall and admired his big brave ideas. But then Alesen was born, and with my maternal juices flowing, I began to see things in a different light.

Our first child was a tiny, serene, peach-colored little girl with big brown eyes. The moment she emerged from my womb she had a quiet look of observation on her face.

Phil was a wonderful adoring father. He did as much for Alesen as I did, except nurse her. His attitude had also begun to change a little. I overheard him tell a friend that he felt more responsible now that he was a father. He said he caught himself driving more cautiously and wasn't quite as daring on skis as he used to be.

23

When our angelic blue-eyed blond Lauri arrived with gusto just a year and a half later, that round-the-world trip lost all its attraction for me. But just as he had been intent on marrying me some day, Phil became more intent upon making that boat dream come true, no matter what. I had hoped time would be on my side and he'd eventually change his mind.

Lauri was only a month old when we bought the *Astrea*. Prior to our first glimpse of this magnificent fifty-two-foot schooner, we had spent many months searching for just the right boat that would fit into Phil's life-long dream. And now with a family included, we needed extra space without sacrificing the look of a sleek, trim vessel.

This was it! We both knew it was love when we sat on deck the very first time. After we were taken for a cruise around the Long Beach Harbor, Phil was hooked. All that I knew of sailboats was what I had learned from looking for one to buy, and in comparison to all we had seen, I was hooked too. Together we agreed to buy her.

The *Astrea* "Goddess of Justice" was the cunning female wedge that began to pry a happy but short-lived marriage apart, and I did not know it. After we bought her, she slowly began to make demands on our time. We discovered a lot of work to be done, over and above the general overhaul and slight remodeling for extra bunks, storage space, and so on.

Many of our weekends were spent apart — Phil worked on the boat and I stayed home with the girls. I could not easily object because we supposedly shared the same goals, and Phil tried to convince me it was a sacrifice well worth making.

He began to look for a crew right away, feeling that if others could be involved in this great effort, then help would be available at all times. He ran ads in the paper and got a huge response. He interviewed every inquirer and followed up on leads about people whom others thought might fill the requirements to be a crew member on this particular kind of trip. Finally, after what Phil thought was great consideration, he chose four men who would furnish their own expenses and sail for the sheer adventure. These were four entirely different personalities, none of which seemed really to blend with the others, but then Phil's primary objective was to find men who were ready, willing, and able — period!

In the deal, Phil got the weekend help he needed to work on the boat, plus two of the fellows alternated staying aboard to work during the week. I joined the work crew whenever I could, but not nearly as much as I would have liked.

When he wasn't working on the boat, Phil was buried in maps, charts, and sailing literature. Out of necessity my attentions were turned toward diapers and meal planning. But Phil was easily transported to the Canary Islands or Fiji as he browsed through his maps and bits of literature, and I would lose him for hours while he sat right there in the same room.

By this time his construction business was booming. He took on his best friend, Dale, as partner and arranged for him to handle the business on the first leg of our trip. Phil was to fly home every six months, then return to continue the voyage.

Plans seemed to be falling into place while we ventured on week-end trips across the channel to Catalina Island. In one year's time these short jaunts were supposed to be for Phil and the crew to learn how to sail the *Astrea* and allow me to get used to the idea of family life afloat. Naturally, we shared some excitement and also suffered some difficulties during this unusual period of adjustment. One unforgettable, horrifying experience became the root of my uncertainty for our future.

One Sunday after a leisurely lunch, we pulled up anchor and headed back toward the mainland when a good sailing breeze came up. We all looked forward to a pleasant and speedy trip home under full sail. As usual, I didn't pay much attention to particulars and just followed my orders to go below to secure the galley and close the port holes. Then we were off. As we headed for Long Beach, we decided to sit on deck, soak up the warm sunshine, and look for another boat to race back with. Instead, the wind shifted and blew from dead ahead, forcing us into a different tack.

As we headed into a strong Santana wind, I went below to make sure the girls would not be tossed around. There was too much sudden commotion on deck, so I thought it best to let the men struggle with the sailing conditions while I attended to the problems below. There was much yelling above me, and I didn't need to be a part of it. I didn't know what was happening on top, but below the girls and I sat huddled in the aft cabin in the corner of a bunk for security.

I heard someone shout that the dinghy was torn loose from the stern, and Phil insisted on turning about to look for it. The wind and waves slammed and crunched the boat. It sounded like we were inside an oil drum as the bow of the boat lifted and then pounded against the sea and shook with thunderous noises. With every crack and thud, I thought the boat would split in half. As the old wooden hull heaved from one side to the other, the sails cracked like rifles and the lines thrashed around the deck like deadly whips.

After about two and one-half hours (the time it would normally take for us to reach the jetty), I strapped the girls in a bunk and went above. When I came out of the hatch, all I could see through the dusty air was a dark sky and an enormous threatening wall of water raised first on one side of the boat and then the other. Voices yelled at Phil who stood frozen and stern at the helm. Much to my surprise the sails were still up.

"Phil," I yelled, "what's the matter?"

He just looked straight ahead and wouldn't speak. Another voice hollered an answer, "He refuses to lower the sails."

"Why?" I yelled back at anyone who would answer.

"He's afraid we won't have enough fuel to get back."

"Oh, no," I said to myself as my heart sank. I knew we were way off course, and we never did find the dinghy. Catalina was out of sight, but so were the landmarks that we usually looked for when we were headed home. I went below to calm the kids. They were frightened, and so was I. They were hungry, too, but it was impossible for me to function in the galley to find something to eat. The hours crawled by. Finally, the girls fell asleep from exhaustion. I strapped each in a lower bunk and then climbed to the one above them. I held firmly to the sides with stiffened arms and braced my feet on the bulkhead. We were still a long way from land. The boat was being tossed about like a small toy, and we made little progress toward safety. I hung on for my life while the cracking and banging pierced my ears and the boat continued to shutter and shake with a clamor. My hair was soaked with tears, and I was afraid we would all soon be swallowed up by the powerful and threatening sea that beat just one plank away from my head. From time to time I was able to lean over and check the girls, amazed that they could sleep so soundly in all the noise. I finally understood the sailor's prayer that was printed on a stainless steel plaque in the main cabin: "O God, thy sea is so great and my boat is so small."

After what seemed like an eon of time, I felt a calm. I couldn't believe it — we were no longer rolling. I pushed myself out of the bunk and slowly headed into the main cabin; someone was asleep, and I ascended the stairs through the hatch. I could see bright stars in the clear black sky above, and Phil stood at the helm. Two of the men sat at the bow smoking cigarettes. The seas were still, and an easy warm and quiet breeze filled the sails. I needed to be with Phil, so I went and stood by his side. I didn't know what to say. He had obviously suffered fear and anxiety himself.

For his sake, I gathered some words and said, "Phil, I think there's some hot coffee in a thermos. Would you like some?"

"Yes," he said. I went below and returned to hand him a steaming cup of black coffee. He took a few sips then spoke quietly.

"I don't know what happened, but I think we can make it now. Are the girls O.K.?"

"Yes," I said in the same quiet mood. "They are sound asleep." Then I admitted I had never been so scared in my life, even though I had experienced some rough flying weather in the past. "But," I continued, "I was not in love with you and two little girls then, either."

At that he set aside the cup of coffee, put one hand on the helm, and with the other pulled me close to his side. "The only thing that kept me sane," he said, "was knowing you and the kids were down below."

29

Then he kissed me, and I saw small pools of water build up in his eyes.

The Long Beach jetty was in sight, and we both heaved a deep sigh of relief. The fear that Phil was not a good sailor left me, and I buried those feelings as we sat there alone in the cockpit with the other woman he loved — his boat.

About a half hour more went by when another gust of wind lashed at us. The new emergency forced us apart. Phil misjudged his position as he turned into the jetty, and the boat was tossed toward the rocks. We felt a horrible crunch as the rocks gouged at the planking. I could see the pain in Phil's face as he fought to clear the boat. We were all so busy we didn't notice the approaching vessel until we heard someone yell through a megaphone from a Coast Guard ship and offer help. Phil refused.

"I'm going to keep the sails up a little longer until I feel I can start the motor and use what fuel we have left to get on into the slip."

The voice from the other ship gruffly ordered, "Put your sails down and start your engine. We'll follow along to help you if you need it."

Phil finally did as he was told, much to our relief, and bravely pulled into our slip before the fuel tank emptied. We stood on deck to wave the Coast Guard off with thanks, then sat in the quiet calm of the marina without saying a word. It had been thirteen hours since we left the island just twenty-three miles ago. Needless to say, the *Astrea* spent some time in dry dock after that trip.

When she returned to the slip and all her wounds were healed, we took one last shake-down cruise to Ensenada, Mexico, another experience which fed my lingering fears and uncertainty. This time, gallons of tequilla fueled the crew. Nevertheless, plans for the final trip continued. Finally, with all the details taken care of, Phil was ready to go. The trip he planned was to have taken four years of our lives.

My job was to stay behind, settle property matters, and sell our belongings while he sailed with the four crewmen to Mazatlan, and I would join them there. I was given my orders as though I were a private expected to report for duty. I tried to be strong, but the full impact really hit home when I watched the *Astrea* glide out of the Long Beach Marina bound for Mexico.

On their day of departure I stood alone on a dock with scrambled feelings. Nearby a gay party of well-wishers had come to send this courageous crew off on their exciting and romantic voyage. I didn't join their merry making because I was sad clear through to my bones.

Before long the *Astrea* was out of sight on the Pacific. The only reality was that I knew I had work to do in a hurry before Phil sent for the girls and me to fly south to meet them.

Dumbfounded, I managed to drive to my sister's house. Susie knew how I felt and let me crawl into a bed where I lay and quietly shivered for hours as my nerves fell completely apart, ending in a heated crying jag. A couple of days passed before I could collect my wits again.

I wanted to trust Phil's plans but was terribly confused as to where I fit into the whole picture. I had never seen a blueprint on marriage, but this wasn't exactly what I thought it should be. On my own I had somehow developed the idea that marriage should be a partnership where two worked as a team. But as I was left behind, I felt more like Phil's caddy while he played the game alone.

By the time his telegram came, I managed to have all the business matters taken care of, and we were packed to go. However, there was one complication: Alesen and Lauri were both in the first stages of the measles. Needless to say, this very untimely delay, combined with the inefficiency of the Mexican telegram system, caused a great deal of communication mix-up and frustration at both ends. My return wire to Phil never reached him, and he had to call from Mexico to find out where I was. Our voices were drowned out in a bad connection, and we never made contact again the whole time we were apart. I had to stay behind a while longer until the measles cleared. Brushing aside my feelings of anxiety, I was sure I'd feel differently once I was in Phil's arms again. The pain of missing him seemed unbearable.

When we were finally able to leave the country, I had to make a decision to fly to Mazatlan and blindly set out somehow to meet Phil. With a friend's knowledge of this Mexican seaport, I figured I'd only have to take a cab to the harbor and look for the *Astrea*. Phil had no way of knowing I was en route, and I had no way of knowing he had not received my wire.

Soon I was in a cab spilling over with excitement at my first view of the harbor. I left the kids in the waiting taxi when I spotted the *Astrea* at the end of a long and rickety dock. Phil was on deck working on some rigging, and I ran to meet him. When he turned to see me coming toward him, his face registered only surprise — not happiness. I didn't care. I just wanted to be in his arms. We called out each other's names, and I ran to receive my welcome kiss. But it was not welcome I felt. I stepped back, sensing I had just kissed a stranger. Phil was a different person.

As if we had never been apart, we exchanged trivialities, and he talked only about the immediate needs for the next leg of the trip — food, water for the tanks, repair for the radio, and a couple of other mechanical items. I couldn't understand him. Had he not missed me, too?

We went back to town with the girls in the cab and checked into a hotel for the night. I was glad to have some privacy before we moved aboard the boat the next day. But Phil was different and seemed only to tolerate my affections. In fact, I was never again to know the comfort and security his arms provided for me in six years of marriage. It was a strange, sleepless night. I lay in bed next to a man who was supposed to be the father of my children but whom I did not know.

IV

WHEN WE JOINED the crew the next day, I learned that Phil had to ask one of them (the youngest) to leave the boat — something about smuggling marijuana and spending time in jail. I never got the story quite straight. The remainder of the crew looked war-torn and lifeless — the same look Phil had. Nobody was glad to see me there. One drop at a time, expectations turned to a tortuous trickle of fear. Perhaps Phil had begun to see the girls and me as a threat to his dream. The boat was in disrepair, and the crew members were unhappy.

We lived on the schooner for three weeks in the harbor at Mazatlan while feelings grew tense for all of us. I found it extremely difficult to set up housekeeping with three other men around all the time. While they did their chores, the girls were a source of irritation to everyone but Phil and me. The engine was torn apart most of the time, and grease was tracked over the beautiful white decks.

We all felt the mounting tension, and there were as many reasons for the discontent and strife as there were people. I resented not having a real family life and home as well as the lack of privacy with my husband. And without coming right out to admit it, the men on board expected me to *prove* I was fit for the jobs assigned to me, besides that of keeping the kids out of everyone's way.

At last Phil insisted that we were ready to push on to the next port, San Blas, and we readied ourselves to set sail. It was good to leave Mazatlan behind. We all needed a change. However, as the *Astrea* glided south, the entire crew experienced a growing cynicism about our adventure. I discovered something that they had obviously felt from the beginning: Phil was not an accomplished sailor. His judgment was questionable in crucial circumstances, and he was unable to delegate the right man to each task. Perhaps the crew was one of the obstacles — I'll never know. Phil just wasn't qualified to take the responsibility for the six other lives aboard his boat, but he was not about to admit it.

For the first time I saw my husband as a mere man, and a pretty weak one at that. He really couldn't walk on water at all. In fact, he couldn't even handle a sailboat. He had hungered such a long time for this trip that it had become an obsession. There was no turning his head to reason, especially after he had gotten as far as a foreign port and tasted adventure and glamour that he never knew before.

After a short stop in San Blas, we set sail for Puerto Vallarta with Phil's hopes blinding him to reality and the crew's tension growing tighter and tighter. Puerto Vallarta was to be our last Mexican stop before heading west toward the islands of the Pacific.

The last remnants of discipline finally broke down among the crew members, and before we reached Puerto Vallarta, all the men except Phil decided to abandon the project.

Puerto Vallarta was breathtaking. I came up from the galley as we slowly pulled in to anchor. The clean white sand arched the edge of a gorgeous wide turquoise bay. Huge emerald mountains leaped up from beaches just behind a sprinkle of quaint thatched-roofed cottages and charming hotels.

We anchored and then all stood on deck to fall in love with this tiny Shangrila we had discovered under a clear blue sky and generous sunshine. For the moment it seemed all our fears and disagreement would melt away until one of the men spoke out to remind us, "This is for me. I'm going to get off and stay right here."

We were met by the harbor master who checked our papers. Then we had lunch aboard, cleaned up a bit, and swam ashore to lie on the beach. Sun bathers swam out to get a closer look at the fantastic schooner that had just pulled in from California.

For days we mixed our damaged relationships and unsettled future plans with a gay whirl of social activity. Most of the crew were finding a wild life on land, and we rarely saw them. They had relinquished what was left of their loyalty and responsibility toward Phil or the boat and did as they pleased. One member, however, was content to stay on board to watch the boat so Phil and I could go ashore for a while.

We found ourselves in the company of wealthy tourists and movie stars who took us under their wing as the "brave and darling young couple on this fabulous yachting adventure." The party life was a merry-go-round, and it didn't take me long to get dizzy. Alcohol was as plentiful as bougainvillea and palm trees. I was tiring rapidly and afraid of all the drinking but could see Phil was winding up — not down. He was enjoying the jet-set life while I waited to find out where we were going from here.

"How long are we supposed to live like this?" I asked him. "I'm getting tired of the late hours at night and mixing booze with sunshine every day." Nor did I appreciate being pawed by strange men and watching Phil get pawed by even stranger women.

He interrupted my sermon to express his feelings, which we were finding little time for. "What difference does it make? No one cares about the boat any more, so I'm going to have a ball while I can."

I let him party alone after that. Alesen and Lauri were becoming lost in the confusion, and I could not stand to do that to them any longer.

When I could take no more, I cried out to Phil, "Get us off this boat. I can't live like this," and continued in frantic emotion. "You can't expect the kids and me to sit back and watch you get drunk every night and sleep it off every day on the beach."

Furious was scarcely the word to describe Phil's reaction. When he opened up, he was extremely violent and vindictive. His crew was leaving, and his wife was part of the mutiny.

Each of the three men found his own reason to desert their captain, and their true motives for making the trip began to emerge. The oldest man, I was told, was running away from an ex-wife who was demanding alimony. He had planned to leave the boat in Australia. After a few days of some socializing, he arranged for a flight to Hawaii and said *adios*.

Another one found a rich American divorcee to drink with and who would treat him to all the luxuries to which he had always wanted to become accustomed. Together they set out for Mexico City and other parts unknown.

The last man seemed to be a little more serious and sober minded about his decision. It took him longer to make his plans. I think he wanted to stick it out, but I overheard him say, "Look, Phil. Make up your mind. Either we set sail, or you set up housekeeping with your family. We can't do both."

And that summed it up. The crew had apparently put the screws to Phil to discourage me from joining them in the beginning. That could explain the reason for his change of attitude toward me. He was caught between two worlds, and his only escape was to drink more. The last crewman returned to the United States a couple of days after his ultimatum.

I was frightened! Here we were in foreign waters, no home to go home to, and our lives in the hands of a very irrational man. He was sure I was the jinx of the project and decided something was mentally wrong with me. He needed someone to blame, and everyone else had scattered. I was all he had left. He said he couldn't face our friends at home and insisted we could *not* give up. His pride hung like a heavy cloud over our lives. Defeat and failure were his demise.

More reckless days went by before Phil saw that I could take no more. He insisted: "Fly home for a couple of weeks and stay with your sister. I'll rent a house in town and keep the girls here." He was dead serious. "Think it through and decide whether or not you trust me. I'll find another crew and get the boat ready." He seemed calm and sure of himself. "I'll wire you when it's time to come back."

In utter confusion and shock, I ached deeply for him. I hated to watch my husband fall apart and was willing to do almost anything to help him through this experience until he could see for himself that he would have to give up his plans. He anticipated my obvious concern and comforted me by saying he had stopped drinking and wouldn't touch another drop.

"That's fine," I said, "but I'd like to take the girls with me."

He came back with an emphatic "No! I think they will be better off here, and it will give you time to rest." Suddenly he showed what seemed like genuine concern and continued to persuade me in a softer tone of voice.

"We'll spend lots of time together and have some fun. It will be good for them, too. They haven't seen much of their daddy lately, and there's so much to see and do here."

Looking for a reason to believe in him once again and wanting to alleviate the pressure we had been under, I flew back to Los Angeles alone. Phil explicitly instructed me not to contact our friends when I got home.

For two weeks I "hid out" at my sister's house in Santa Ana. Being without my family was like being without my arms. The days crawled by and not one word from Mexico. Every moment was filled with anticipation of hearing from Phil and hoping against hope that he would change his mind and come on home too.

I wrote daily, mostly directed to the girls so they would not think I had abandoned them. I never knew until much later that my letters were unopened and thrown away upon arrival, for my name or any reference to "mommy" was never discussed in my absence.

In spite of Phil's definite instructions, I felt an urgency about calling his partner, Dale. I would just let him know I had come back alone for a while and ask him to keep it to himself. But I had to know if he had heard from Phil. The timing was miraculous.

"What are you doing here?" he asked with alarm. "I just got a wire from Phil, and he said he's leaving tomorrow for Tahiti. He's just waiting for me to send some money."

While he waited for my answer, I froze, and the phone felt as if it were welded to my ear. I could not move.

Then the fog lifted, and the picture was all too clear. It terrified and angered me. Phil had no intention of having me return to Vallarta. He knew when I left what he would do, and I was not to be included in his plans.

My heart shattered into a million pieces, and hot tears boiled out of my eyes as I tried to speak. I finally realized there was no more room to trust this stranger that I called my husband.

"Don't send the money, Dale! Please!" I begged. "The girls are down there with him. I can't let him take them on the boat." When I told Dale the whole ugly story, he agreed with me 100 percent that I should return for Alesen and Lauri immediately, and he helped me arrange to leave.

Having confirmed our hasty plans, I slumped and let the receiver fall from my ear. Susie grabbed the phone to pick up the details of the situation, and her eyes widened at hearing what was going on. Since she was the only other person to know what was happening, she too began to cry but tried to comfort me.

"Everything will be all right," she said. But she knew I was being crushed, and there were no comforting words. She hung up the phone and turned to me where I sat on her bed.

"Susie," I screamed, "why has he done this thing? Why?" I threw myself face down on the bed and clawed like a wildcat at her bedspread, shredding some parts of it with my fingernails.

I thought I would lose my mind as I cried bitter and hate-filled tears. Finally exhausted, I knew I would have to compose myself in order to fly back to Mexico for the girls. Their safety was all that mattered now.

Making that trip back alone was unthinkable in my state of mind. Susie insisted on going with me, and I was somewhat relieved when her husband agreed and said he would help all he could. Early the next morning we drove to Los Angeles and boarded our plane with return tickets in my purse.

The trip seemed to last an eternity. We discussed little else but how we would quickly find the girls and get them away from Phil as soon as possible. How naive we were.

When we arrived in Vallarta, I recognized two young beach boys in the airport lobby. They acknowledged my return as their faces registered surprise. A few words in Spanish passed between them before they scurried out, tossing a sly grin our way. We did not know that they had gone ahead to announce our arrival.

It was some time before we could get a cab. When we did, the driver seemed to be deliberately taking his time as he taxied us into town.

"I feel like we're about to walk into a trap," I told Susie.

"I have the same feeling," she said and asked the driver why he had to go so slowly. He did not answer but stared straight ahead. The silence of the driver was our eerie companion in that cab as it slowly rattled down dirt roads through the humid jungle country toward the main section of town.

When we finally reached our destination, it seemed as if huge brown eyes were staring at us wherever we walked. We had to ask around to find out where Phil (known as the captain of the big boat) and the girls were living. Not many people were anxious to help us. We walked down to the beach, hoping to find them there, but it became apparent that Phil's plans to sail without me were well known. His Mexican friends were not eager to help me locate him.

In spite of all the quiet responses, we finally got enough information to take us directly to where the girls were playing just outside the little rented house. With an insight into Phil's twisted, new personality, I was relieved to see that the girls did not look neglected.

Alesen and Lauri were ecstatic with screams and giggles when they saw me with their Auntie Susie. I swept them into my arms and clung to them for dear life.

"What was I thinking to ever leave you down here?" I mumbled in their hair while I kissed their heads and cheeks. "I'll never leave you again," I cried. They were happy and healthy looking from spending every day on the beach.

A young Mexican girl came out of the house and asked in very poor English, "Are you their *mamasita*?" I assured her that I was and found out she was taking care of them for a while. "Señor Hayes will be back pretty soon," she said as she leaned against the door so that we could not enter.

I was sure that by now Phil knew we had come to town and it would be just a matter of minutes before I'd see him. In even less time than I thought, Phil pulled up along the curb in a jeep. His informants made him all too aware that I had not returned to continue a boat trip with him, and I had no interest in confronting him to try to change his mind.

In her anger Susie spoke up: "We're taking Alesen and Lauri back home where they belong."

From that moment on it was war. Phil tried every verbal trick possible to stall us and displayed great hostility and bitterness. While Susie went into the house to find the girls' belongings, Phil threatened that I would not be able to take the children out of Mexico without his permission. I could not see how that was possible since they were on my passport and I held all the necessary papers.

Susie and I had been there longer than we wanted to already. When she came downstairs with a small suitcase, Phil angrily peeled the jeep away from the curb, rounded the corner leaving a cloud of dust in his wake. Now I was scared and felt the sooner we could leave, the better, and quickly found a cab.

With Alesen and Lauri in hand we piled into the back seat and headed for the airport. On the way, however, we were stopped by the Mexican police. The next thing I knew I was being dragged to jail and all my legal papers were taken from me.

Someone pushed my sister back into the cab and told the driver to take her on to the airport. I glanced at her face to see the reflection of terror as she was spun away down the street — helpless!

It looked as if Phil had won not only the first round, but the entire battle of this horrid struggle.

V

NOW STANDING ON THE BALCONY gazing out at the bay, I noticed the sky turned pink while the sun lowered itself into the sea. I heard a voice call, "Señora, señora." My eyes floated to the street below. A young man was trying to get my attention.

"You want me?" I asked.

"*Si*! Are you Señora Hayes?"

"Yes," I answered, once again fully aware of my present surroundings.

"I have a letter here from your seester," he announced.

With that I ran downstairs to get some lead on Susie's safety.

"Your seester gave me one dollar and told me to make sure I geeve theese to you and no one else."

I thanked him several times, closed the front door for privacy, ripped open the envelope, and recognized her handwriting. What a relief to know she had gotten on the plane safely. She enclosed ten dollars and instructed me to wire her of my safety as soon as possible. Since I did not know at that point if I was, in fact, safe, I decided to wait a day or so and stuffed the envelope deep into a pocket.

The still, quiet moments passed slowly while I waited for a sign of Phil and the girls. For the first time, I took inventory of my surroundings. In the tropical heat, the dust flew around at the mere whisper of a breeze. The country had not yet been turned green by the storms that were on their way. My brown-skinned neighbors sauntered back and forth seemingly without direction or purpose — almost as if their slow movements would cool them off.

The house and neighborhood, old and historical, consisted of the barest necessities. Here I sat in a rented two-story house squeezed into a small area between two other buildings. I noticed it had lots of room in all the wrong places, with the traditional indoor patio and a kitchen as an afterthought.

At last Phil walked through the door with our daughters at his side and a look of total defeat on his face. We were both grieved for our own reasons and didn't trust the other enough to let down for a second.

We remained in Puerto Vallarta for several weeks, and I watched my husband disintegrate into a madman, grasping at straws to keep his plans together. I rarely saw him, for he had gathered around him a circle of seedy friends, both Mexican and American, who were supposedly helping him get the boat and crew ready to sail. I had obviously thrown a monkey wrench in the previous plans and new arrangements had to be made.

I was helpless — he had all the papers I needed to leave the country — so I just waited and lived every day in fear of my life.

An entirely different person, Phil was now doing things beneath any human decency. The obvious problems were his heavy drinking and too many hints of some kind of drug. One of his new companions was the woman who took Alesen and Lauri from me at the jail, and Phil didn't mind being intimate with her in my presence. I knew he would still try to take the girls from me the minute I turned my back.

One day he came up behind me on the beach. He stood and gingerly removed the foil wrapping from a tiny piece of cake. Shoving it at my face, he demanded, "Here! I want you to taste this. It's the best banana cake I've ever had."

Backing away from his hand in dismay, I told him I didn't want any cake.

"Take this and eat it!" He screeched the words out between his teeth.

Feeling brave only because of the crowd around us, I looked defiantly into his eyes and said, "I won't eat that or anything else you give me." As I spoke, I saw that his violent eyes were red where the white should have been.

Looking from side to side and noticing the staring sun bathers all around, he was easily discouraged and walked away, still handling that little piece of cake as if it were a precious stone. I suspected, of course, that he was trying to drug me.

I barely slept nights, and eating became a real chore. My only concern was to keep the girls busy and out of Phil's reach. He was swiftly going mad. I was constantly on the look-out for strangers, never knowing what he planned to do next. As much as possible, I guarded the girls from the fear that was raging in me. I trusted no one and waited as patiently as possible for some move from Phil.

Weird whispered meetings occurred at all hours of the night downstairs while I was supposedly sleeping. It was scary to wait for the final outcome of all those sneaky rendezvous.

Phil even made a quick trip back to Los Angeles to get some more money, leaving the impression with his envious friends that all was going well and the trip was continuing beautifully. Meanwhile, I was still in Mexico with someone watching my every move. I was later informed that the man Phil had hired to watch me was armed and had been instructed to shoot if I tried to leave the country.

After weeks of just trying to keep tabs on the girls and watching out every second for my own safety, Phil finally gave up his end of the struggle and said the girls and I could return to the states. I had no idea what he had been up to or with whom he had been spending each long day. I didn't ask any questions; I just waited for a trickle of instruction.

I was stunned when he gave me the passports, plane tickets, and fifty dollars and released himself from any further responsibility for me and his daughters. He simply informed me that he and his new crew members, whom I had never seen, would leave for Tahiti in a few days. I didn't ask any questions and kept my emotional guard up.

For weeks Phil had been a total stranger to me, but suddenly he began to soften back into the person I once knew. It was as if someone had cut the strong wire of tension between us. We were able to spend an entire day together just talking, he and I. The transition was remarkable and left me almost vulnerable.

Our conversation flowed into reviewing the love and hope we had known together just a few months before. I never once questioned his decision during this time, however, because I did not want to disturb the first breath of peace since we arrived in Mexico. Though I still could not dredge up any remnants of trust, I came to a point of at least hoping that things would eventually turn out O.K. when this was out of his system.

"If I could just get as far as Tahiti . . ." he said hopefully, "then we could work on getting our marriage back to normal again."

Our last night together melted into a real union of need and love for each other. For a few brief hours we were the only two people in the whole world, and being together was all that ever mattered. Then finally we slept peacefully as one for the last time.

The next morning, however, reminded me all too abruptly that Phil was still going on with his plans. I was upstairs getting dressed, hypnotically going through the motions of checking passports, tickets, and baggage — such as it was — when I heard the voices of my family downstairs. In her feminine inquiring tone of voice, four-year-old Alesen said, "But, daddy, why don't you come on the airplane with us?"

My stomach churned, and my heart waited to explode as he answered. "Because . . ." he paused a second to swallow, ". . . I'm going to sail the *Astrea* to the other side of the ocean, darling, and I may not see you again for a long time."

His answer was as matter of fact as if it was one of life's routines she must learn to accept — like brushing her teeth. I can't remember whether the tone of regret I heard was in his voice or in my imagination. Quietly I descended halfway down the steep staircase to take in the picture below for what I did not realize would have to last me for the rest of my life.

My tanned, well-built, once handsome, loving husband sat with our two daughters — one on each knee — telling them good-by. ". . . and I want you both to promise daddy you will let your hair grow so that when I see you again it will be clear down your back." I thought he was exaggerating a bit as he marked an imaginary line in the middle of their backs. "That will be our way of measuring time between now and when I see you again."

As I walked the rest of the way down the stairs with a forced smile of anticipation for the airplane trip, Phil looked up suddenly to realize he had made a dreadfully wrong decision. He held in his arms the two wonderful little girls he had watched come into this world, and he was in love with his wife who loved him in return. Unable to hold back any longer, he half-yelled with a crack in his voice and pleaded, "Oh, God! What am I doing? I must be out of my mind to let the most beautiful wife and family leave me."

Yet it was difficult to determine who was leaving whom. My husband had a boyhood dream of someday sailing his own luxurious vessel around the world. Tragically, the time came when he had to decide if that boyhood dream was worth fulfilling, even at the risk of losing people he loved.

As I reached the bottom of the stairs, Phil rose to his feet. For the first time in our life together I could see only the shell of a man I had once looked up to with such faith and admiration as my pillar of strength — my god. Knowing we were still a part of each other, I could not resist his touch one last time and slowly went to him to take in the feel of his strong muscular arms. His arms opened to me, and I leaned on his bare shoulder and kissed his neck and lips — desiring to drink of him all I could before we parted.

He gently held me in his arms until the taxi arrived, and it seemed the driver deliberately blew the horn long and loud to dismantel our emotions. Turning from me to the girls while gathering all the strength in his soul, he kneeled to say, "Be good girls on the airplane and mind your mommy so you can all enjoy your trip, O.K.?"

"O.K., daddy," they replied without sadness.

"Lemme kiss you, daddy!" came a request from the beaming little face of two-year-old Lauri. Both girls scrambled to be swooped up in their daddy's arms.

There was nothing more for us to say to each other. We knew the longing to be together would last, and we knew we had exhausted all the avenues of words and actions.

The girls hurried into the cab, and I followed with a hollow in my soul — determined to be strong so that the children would not catch the true sadness and heartbreak of this parting. Still, nothing was said. Only the girls chattered questions as Phil handed the taxi driver our bags. Climbing into the cab, I looked back through the rear window to see my love — my husband, my life — standing alone, listless and burdened with his own sadness.

This tower of a man had dwindled to a mere lost figure through a decision to do what we both feared but did not want to realize: to sail to a goal of death at sea.

Still reaching out with our hearts, we looked at each other while the cab pulled away from the sidewalk. I will always remember seeing him for the last time through the dust kicked up by the turning wheels of the taxi. He stood bare-chested, dressed only in a pair of worn Levis, his thumbs hung on his back pockets, and tears streamed down his lifeless face. Then the taxi turned the corner.

All I could feel was the yearning to be by his side. My heart wanted me to turn around and go back to him, but intuition silenced me and held me firmly in the back seat of that rumbly old taxi cab as it made its way out of town on that familiar road toward the airport.

I watched the girls and wondered if these two children, who now monopolized every second with their anxious movements and shrilly, excited voices, would really ever see their daddy again in their lifetime. Would Phil be with them as they grew into young ladies as he so often talked about and looked forward to?

At last we boarded the plane, but I wasn't sure I could breathe easily until we touched down in Los Angeles. I was right. As if I had not tasted enough bitter panic and fear, I was handed another dose of it upon leaving Mazatlan, the customs stop before entering the United States.

Mexican officials held me back of the line as the other passengers reboarded the plane for the last half of the trip. The gate closed with finality at the exit, and once again I was being questioned by the Mexican authorities. They informed me in their broken English that they had found marijuana in my luggage. "We'll have to take your children and keep you in custody overnight at the police stasheon," they concluded.

I threw a glance outside the gate as I heard the roar of the plane's engines start at that moment. I wanted to scream, but I knew they would carry me away to an insane asylum. I searched the lobby for a friendly American face. There was no one.

"Oh, God! What now?" I said aloud as I closed my eyes to shut out the pain for just an instant. Immediately from somewhere down inside me came a surge of power that was certainly beyond my own, and with it came an amazing escape story. I had not the time to *think* about what was going to come from my mouth and was shocked with every word. The timing was absolutely perfect. I could not have planned it.

"I don't know what you *think* you have found. You can *keep* the luggage," I commanded. "But do you see those two little girls over there?" pointing to Alesen and Lauri skipping around the empty lobby. He turned and spotted them.

"One of them will die of a serious disease within twenty-four hours unless we are back in Los Angeles today where a doctor is awaiting our return to take us to a hospital."

The story was brilliant, but I continued with amazement, "Does the Mexican government want that on their heads?"

I'm sure he did not know that I was as startled as he, and he replied hurriedly, "No, Señora, no, no!" He signaled with all kinds of motions to the other officers at the desk, and I was rushed through the gates. I called Alesen and Lauri to hurry and get back on the plane. They obeyed anxiously and were at my side at once.

To this day I don't understand *how* it happened, but I now know *where* that story came from. How often and loosely we call on the One who wants to help us, and when we receive that help, we immediately forget where it came from.

"Just a minute, lady." A young Mexican officer had followed after us and took the opportunity to make one more threat. "You give us whatever dollars you have in your purse and then you can go."

Alesen tugged at my dress, and Lauri fought to keep my hand as I reached for my wallet. The engine roar was deafening and made me extremely nervous. But fifty dollars and thirty seconds later we were boarding the plane again — just a split-second before the ramp fell away. The door closed, and the aircraft started down the runway before we could find our seats.

I don't remember breathing for the remainder of the trip home, and I waited with my fists clenched for something else to keep us from safety. Was that just one last trick of Phil's to keep me from leaving? I wondered.

Suspicious of every one on the plane, I froze when a tall, well-dressed Mexican businessman stooped in front of my seat. I quickly looked at his eyes but would not believe what I saw. Is that concern and compassion? I thought. No, impossible! I don't really know what that is any more.

"Are you all right?" he asked, and I stiffly shook my head yes.

"Can I get you something?" I shook my head no.

"I saw what happened back there." He spoke beautiful English, packaged with all the charm of a young cosmopolitan attorney, but I turned away in distrust.

"They take advantage of women alone." Not wanting to talk to him, I stared blindly past his face, but he continued, "I just wanted to let you know I was praying for you."

When I looked once again at his face, he rose and walked away.

VI

THE GIRLS AND I arrived at the Los Angeles airport bringing only what we were wearing. My luggage was still in Mazatlan, along with all the money I had. Having no other choice in the matter, I searched the line of passengers for that one kind man and asked him for a dime. "I need to call and have someone pick us up," I explained.

"I understand," he said. And I was grateful he didn't continue in conversation. My major objective was to find a telephone. Dale answered after the first ring, and I was relieved.

"We just arrived in L.A.," I blurted out. I thought I would pass out from exhaustion and closed my eyes, longing for a soft place to lie down. "Can you pick us up? I'll tell you all about it later."

"I'm glad to hear you're all right," he said calmly. "I'll be right there." He was about forty minutes away. Being considerate of my sister, he added, "Before I leave here, I'd like to call Susie and let her know that you're safe and sound."

Safe and sound? Little did he know!

I collected the girls and walked slowly to the main lobby where Dale was to meet us. I sat in a chair and lost myself in time and space while Alesen and Lauri played and skipped around the flight insurance booths.

Back in the hustle of American living, people scurried back and forth in total freedom, darting busily around as if they were chasing each other. Did they know how fortunate they were? A brief sense of security welled up inside me, and I was grateful to be back in a country where the protection of its citizens is of utmost importance. Just hours before, I had been suspect smuggler in a foreign country. Now here I sat completely unnoticed in the midst of huge crowds.

As my thoughts drifted and noise drowned out the present, I wondered, What happened to the girl whose life had been full of promise, whose past was looked upon with envy as she flew around the country on her stewardess wings? What happened to the young man whose ambition and zest for living was sure to bring him success? What happened to the bright future of those two people who were married just six years ago and destined to be the pacesetters for victorious young marrieds?

What now? What's the purpose for all this? Is this the summation of life?

I had asked myself at least one-hundred times, What is life for anyway? And each time the answers seemed further and further away: unreachable.

Dale's soft, quiet voice broke the spell. "Hi. Where are the girls?"

I looked up into the first trustworthy face I had seen in a very long time. "They're over there," and I pointed to a booth where Alesen and Lauri sat to watch all the busy people. He looked toward two very tanned but skinny and tired little girls who were not strangers to him.

All the way home I slowly filled Dale in on the details. He had a thousand questions. Phil was his best friend, and he was as hurt by the change in his nature as I was. Though I had gone through those nightmare weeks with Phil, it was almost as hard for me to believe as it was for Dale.

"Susie wants you and the girls to stay at her house until you find out what's happening," he said.

After arriving at my sister's, I went through the awful experience again, this time spilling myself out in a flow of sobbing and tears as if a plug had been pulled. After that I think I slept for two days solid.

VII

UNDER NORMAL SAILING CONDITIONS, it takes about fifteen to eighteen days to cross the ocean between the Mexican coastline and the Pacific islands.

Once again Phil wired Dale his plans to set sail for Tahiti. He said he had picked up a new crew and would need money upon arriving in Pepeete. Dale was cautious. He decided to wait and make sure Phil had actually arrived before sending any money.

We waited intently for two and one-half weeks — no word. Allowing for possible minor delays, we waited a little longer. Inquiries to the Port Captain in Pepeete returned negative. Finally, after six weeks, Dale took measures to contact the Coast Guard.

Phil's disappearance hit the news media. Subcontractors on his jobs, justly concerned, were forced to put liens on all the buildings still under construction. Hayes Construction Company was falling apart, and it was obvious I could not depend on the business for financial support. Dale was grasping at loose ends in an effort to glean a little support for his family, too. Faced with the problem of law suits, he had to close down all the jobs. We suffered a great financial loss.

My "struggle for survival" began with having to fill out applications for a secretarial job. Marital status: Married? Single? Divorced? Widow? I'm not single or divorced, I thought. If I were married, I wouldn't be filling out this crummy application, and I refuse to check widow.

The confusion often sent me walking away from an interview discouraged. How could I explain my situation when I didn't understand it myself? My qualifications were desirable, but my marital status, whatever that was, made me a poor employment risk.

One day I braved the business world again, armed with the decision simply to lie and offer an explanation to no one. I checked "single with two dependents" and began my first job with a large company in Newport Beach.

My heart wasn't in my work, however. The girls were in nursery school, and I felt my real job was to be with them. I will be eternally indebted to Mrs. Petties, a beautiful little woman who ran the nursery school and provided the love and stability for my children that I was unable to give them for a long, long time.

I found a small apartment near my sister's home in Santa Ana and tried to set up housekeeping after work and on weekends. The confusion of my situation surfaced after a couple of weeks on the job, however, as other employees innocently asked questions to learn more of the new secretary in the office. Eventually, my boss called me into his office to find out more about the rumors of my mysterious life. With some sense of relief I began my story and tried to keep it simple, but his curiosity generated question after question, and I became a little emotional. I knew my job depended on my reaction, so I did my best to keep cool and calm. His compassionate response took me by surprise, and I felt grateful that he let me keep my job after knowing I was living under very trying circumstances.

Dale understood the strain I was under. Sensitive to my brittle emotions, he shielded me from much of the debris that was bound to surface. He only informed me about those things that would be of some relief or help. We were in constant contact and discovered that Phil's new crew was four young Americans who were apparently willing to sail as far as Tahiti with plans to fly home after a brief stay.

Though Dale tried his best to protect me from the flack of news-seekers, the families of Phil's new crew filtered through to me for further information, which I could not give them. They wanted to believe I could throw some light on the subject, but they knew as much if not more than I did.

Some weeks later I learned that the Coast Guard had searched thoroughly for the *Astrea* and had filed the longest incomplete search report in history. Dale told me that the United States Navy was also commissioned to search the Pacific Ocean in the areas of possible shipwreck, and one of the families launched a private search as well. Finally, on October 30, more than four months after I had left Phil in Mexico, all official search for the *Astrea* and her crew was called off. Both the Navy and the Coast Guard had found nothing after weeks of retracing the *Astrea's* probable course. These fragments of evidence were all I had to live on.

Meanwhile, I plunged head first into the business of earning a living. I continually tried to decide whether or not I was a widow and wondered constantly if and when Phil would suddenly reappear on the scene of our lives. I began to look for him in every passing car on the road, around every corner. Despair became my daily companion, but I knew I could not maintain my job if I allowed fear to consume me.

My boss's compassion for my problem spilled over into lunch invitations, which I naively accepted, only to learn the hard way that my job depended on how much attention I was willing to give him "after hours" too. I thought he was joking. A few days later I learned he wasn't; so I walked out — nauseated.

With a bitter taste in my mouth, but a little tougher skin, I found another job. The days were difficult , but the nights were unendurable. Lonely and frightened, I lay awake watching the girls as they slept and wondering why they were ever allowed to be born.

"Where is their daddy?" I cried. "Why did he leave? What can I tell them that they can understand at their very young age?" My crumbled heart felt like scattered pebbles in my chest. They just don't deserve the tragedy of having to live out this life, I pondered.

They are so precious to me, but what can I do for them?

Those last bitter weeks in Mexico were relived as I tried to figure out what I might have said or done that would have altered the whole picture. I blamed myself for the turn of events in our marriage and built up a tremendous self-guilt.

All the while I received phone calls from the relatives of Phil's crew. They lashed out at me for their missing sons and accused me of being involved in a plot to do away with the lives of people they loved. "You're going to collect some insurance money from the boat and meet Phil somewhere in the South Pacific!" they declared.

I needed some one, some thing, to hang onto that would give me hope for the future. It seemed that even my family let me down when I reached out to them. I did not understand that what I needed could not be obtained from any human being. No one had an answer to help me. I met people in the business world but generally left them behind at 5:00 P.M. when I picked up my girls from nursery school and went home.

Those people were not a part of my *real* life with my children, nor did I want them to be, for I was still keeping house for a husband who never came home.

VIII

MY SOCIAL LIFE was absolutely zero. Yet all the books and magazines I read seemed to advise me to "swing," "live it up," "have a ball!"

"Is that what I need?" I asked a girl in my office.

"Sure," she said, "I know lots of guys who would like to get to know you better."

Utter loneliness drove me to accept a few invitations to dinner from various men — only to come home and look back on the evening as a waste of time. The men I dated conversed in trivialities; they had nothing to say that I needed or wanted to hear. I quickly tired of the same old drippy line of clumsy compliments and praises to my "beauty, intelligence, and sex appeal." The follow-up was always the same — a confession that they just couldn't "control" themselves any longer...

Most of their approaches were corny and insincere, and I wasn't the least bit interested. It's a game, a foolish game, I thought. My heart and mind easily drifted back to the whereabouts of the *Astrea* and her crew, right in the middle of a conversation over martinis. Consequently, I rarely dated the same man twice. I was considered a "dud."

All too soon I became aware that half the men I dated were married and that all I meant to them was something they could get their kicks with while their wives weren't looking. I knew this type of life was going on somewhere but never thought I'd be a part of it. Disgusted with my new life-style, my only defense was to build a wall of distrust for *every* man I met.

What's it all about? I asked again and again. Finally, I justified the circumstances by telling myself, So what if they're married. Basically so was I. Then I settled my inward struggle by deciding marriage was a farce. After all, look where mine left me.

After a lengthy training period, I became quite expert at playing my role in this so called night life, and I determined to be the greatest thing to come down the pike. No one was going to call me a dud any more. I knew I couldn't get emotionally involved with any other man; yet if I was truly a widow, I hoped against hope that one day some man would enter my life and offer all that I felt entitled to — love, security, riches, and so on. I deserve a free meal, I told myself. If I don't take advantage of it, they'll just get someone else. I knew they had more to lose than I did, so I rationalized, Why not?

Then I discovered a world of men who would rather buy me a fifth of bourbon than pay my baby-sitter. And, oh, the loneliness of a smoke-filled bar lined with "the beautiful people" of the business jet set. After the third martini, the masks of innocent innuendos were tossed aside, and the "real man" emerged to make his final play.

"Oh, Phil," I cried out when I got home, "why did you leave me to fight this battle alone?" Once again I retreated into a shell, wondering, Where in the world do I belong? Soon I concluded that the world and God, whoever and wherever he was, had given me the dirty end of the stick. With this I decided to get back all I could to replace what I had lost, so I skimmed through my working days and hung on to my night life. There was no alternative.

I was very discriminating, I thought, for I only dated men who could afford me. I went to all the best restaurants, drove in the finest cars, and was seen with the most dapper men to let the world know I wasn't going to be cast aside so easily. Though I knew I was fighting a losing battle, I was offered champagne and glitter. That was the best there was, so I took it all. Never satisfied, I moved from one job to another and from one rented place to another, each time seeking some means of security. It was a long way off.

My next step was to learn all the right drinks to order before dinner, the right wines to drink with dinner, the right things to say during dinner, and finally the right things to do after dinner to play my end of that filthy game called "Let's Cheat."

I began to identify with the Playboy philosophy, which became my way of life. It was satisfying to know an entire magazine not only approved of my life-style but encouraged me as well. Lenny Bruce became my idol. I could easily relate to this desperately honest man who cried out for love and understanding and yet lashed back with harsh truths of man's inhumanity to man.

There was a struggle going on deep down inside that was dirty and constantly with me. I spent a great deal of time in the shower after the baby-sitters left. I thought if I scrubbed hard enough I could get clean *inside* and out.

To whom among my temporary friends could I admit my feelings of insecurity and guilt? Their immediate reaction would have been, "Wow, you really have a lot of hangups." Consequently, I could only adhere to the philosophy: I can do anything I want to as long as I don't hurt anybody.

My life was going from bad to worse, nevertheless, and I knew all too well that it was the same life my mother struggled with for a while as a single woman. It's the same life so many are left to live with in search of a reason for being. The night spots may have been a little classier, but the stench was just as foul. Alesen and Lauri were witnesses to that. On one occasion when I returned home late, the baby-sitter left, and I went in to check the girls as they slept soundly. My heart swelled up into my throat, and tears of shame poured down my face. I kneeled down beside Alesen's bed and woke her up with some alcoholic kisses and wet cheeks, combined with the smell of tobacco smoke in my hair and clothes. She tried to move her head away from me as she said sleepily, "Oooh, mommy — you stink!"

72

Yes, I did stink and was helpless to do anything about it except head for the shower which could not provide the cleansing I needed so desperately. How sickening that I should afflict my beautiful young daughters with the woman I was becoming.

IX

ALMOST TWO CONFUSING and wasted years crawled by between the time I got off a plane with two little girls and the time I decided to take my own life. The only memories I held of the past were horrible and full of pain. The family life I had wanted for years was nonexistent, and the future didn't look any brighter; so my plans to commit suicide seemed very practical. Life was totally senseless. Death just had to be an improvement. My philosophy wasn't working, for I had hurt other people in my quest for meaning to life.

One Friday night I drove the girls out of town to spend the weekend with some relatives. There were plans of fun and entertainment in store for them, and I was relieved because I surely could not provide much. I dropped them off, gave them each a big hug and kiss, and headed back to the apartment I loosely called home. It was dark, and as I opened the door, I suddenly stepped into a daze of total emptiness. The apartment was void of sound and movement. My own life and breath vanished into the hollowness. In a stupor, I sat on the couch and stared into the darkness without seeing, hearing, or feeling anything. The only glaring reminder of my existence was the one simple but giant question that filled my head — *why*?

Sometime much later that night I quietly and simply planned a way of escape. I searched the medicine cabinet and mixed a handful of sleeping pills and aspirin. There was no question that I would take the next step; it was just a matter of when. As if I was not in control, I waited for the mechanism in my arms to reach for a glass of water and raise the pills to my mouth. But then I thought of calling my father.

"I just want to say hi," I said aloud. And the sound of my own voice made me conscious of what I was about to do. I cried blinding tears but made no sound. Then I got mad at myself because of my stupid sudden desire to call my dad. I wanted a quick exit from all my thoughts, so I darted toward the kitchen sink, filled a glass with water, and shoved a bunch of dry, bitter pills into my mouth.

Without regret I stood in the small apartment kitchen for a moment and wondered how much time it would take until my life would be x'd out. I contemplated for a while longer when all of a sudden I thought of the girls. Who should keep them? I think I dizzily wrote a note of instructions for my family as to what Alesen's and Lauri's individual needs were and with whom they should live. In the time that it took me to write the note several times over, I began to get drowsy, so I sat down to wait it out. Then in an even drowsier state I reached for the phone and dialed my dad's number. I don't remember much after that except that I wanted to lie down. When I heard my dad's voice on the line, all I could slur together was, "Hi, pop — I'm so tired." Then I phased out.

When I woke in a mental hospital, it was Susie's face I saw in the light, and I knew I had flubbed my attempt. I closed my eyes and wished I would never have to open them again to face my sister, whom I had included in one of my selfish games and whom I had hurt deeply. Nevertheless, it was my sister who helped to launch me back into the reality of living again. She visited me in the hospital, encouraged me to keep going for Alesen's and Lauri's sake, and she took care of them until I could be released and on my feet again. I will be forever grateful for her love and forgiveness to me at that time.

My sloppy attempt to overdose on some pills resulted in a police report and a brief stay in the county hospital. Release was contingent on the results of a series of sanity tests, from which they discovered I was my own worst enemy. But inside the hospital I was the chosen enemy of a young Mexican girl who had been there for several weeks. One night I woke suddenly when she held a pillow tightly over my face. I managed to squirm loose with a scream, and the orderlies pulled her off. She had a private room after that, and I never saw her again.

My release did not mean freedom, for hard as I tried not to, I landed smack back into the rut I was in before: too many men, too much alcohol, too many meaningless philosophies, and too little time with my children.

The worst thing of all was that I found nothing in life worth passing on to Alesen and Lauri.

X

THE GIRLS AND I struggled through several more moves before we found a house for rent in a beautiful little town near the beach. I thought for sure that this was where I could really start all over again. Corona del Mar was the place we'd call home at last and find the peace and tranquillity I longed for. But even with the best intentions, I kept stumbling into my past and ended up in the same routine: the highly competitive business world, phoney dinner dates, meaningless weekends, loneliness, and bitter memories.

I was not prepared when a young man entered my life who seemed honestly to care about me and the girls. He took me by surprise. By this time, I was cold and extremely hard and bitter, but he was warm and had strong "naive" convictions about morals and honesty. I secretly liked what he said, but I laughed at him and was determined to prove I didn't need anyone. He was just as determined to prove otherwise.

He was younger than I and not yet scarred too badly by life's ugly offerings. One of his tender tools to break me was his sincere concern for Alesen and Lauri. He would stop by at night to tuck them snugly in bed with a kiss and ask how their day went at school. I finally began to look upon him as a potential "someone" I could trust.

He hammered at my resistance with his consistent love and concern for the three of us. He liked to fix things around the house, and to a single woman, a find like this is a real treasure. He even offered to babysit with the girls while I went off on some tangent to "find myself" in intellectual pursuits — adult college courses, meditation groups, philosophy, Eastern religion, sensitivity groups, and so on. I had to find some handle to hang on to in order to keep going.

In my heart I knew this man had the flavor of decency I once had. He wanted to get married, but I couldn't understand marriage any more, not after all the marriages in which I had been a third person. "Besides that," I argued with resentment, "I don't know if I'm a widow or not." Nevertheless, his love for us grew stronger, and my feelings for him too felt more and more like love.

In order to keep from being hurt again, I justified the love I felt and suggested a compromise. "Can't we just pretend we're married?" I asked. "I think I could handle that." We went away for a few days, and when we returned, our "marriage" was announced to friends and families.

He tried desperately to make it work out. He was willing to take on the responsibility of protecting me and raising my children, but I could not afford to let him love us. "You'll leave for greener pastures some day," I said. And the fear that he would scared me to death. This man was willing to care for me when I was ill, love and discipline my children, and cradle me with comfort through my frequent nightmares. I didn't mind any love he could show the girls, but I stepped between them when he started the discipline.

"You're not their father," I screamed, as if it was his fault. I didn't know or care that it would be impossible to expect him to love them without discipline too. Nor did I realize that proper discipline was an indication of love. All I did was scream at them a lot.

My nightmares were always the same: full of fear and guilt about Phil's disappearance. In an effort to help me finalize Phil's death, this man spent an entire day with the Long Beach Coast Guard, combing through the search report. Having a love and respect for the ocean and sailing himself, he understood the nautical descriptions about the tides, currents, and weather conditions. He anxiously came home to tell me what the records revealed: the all-too-slim possibility that the *Astrea* could have even survived the conditions that prevailed in the Mexican waters at the time of her departure. His efforts were in vain. I wanted to know the impossible, and nothing else would satisfy me. My deep feelings for this man had to be guarded from hurt at all cost; so even though I was grateful, I showed no gratitude.

After about a year and a half of treating him with cruel indifference, I could not stand living with myself or with him any longer. I had lived enough lies, but now I lived a lie to my children and to his parents, whom I loved as much as I was capable of loving anyone.

Disgusted with the business world, and aching to escape once more, I had a chance to fly again. I heard of a new local airline that was hiring ex airline personnel, whether single, married, or with children, as long as they had previous experience. I grabbed the opportunity in order to elevate my life-style and seek some other purpose for my existence, but it didn't work. I tried to maintain two lives by keeping my home life a secret at work. When I wasn't flying, I played at being a "wife and mother." When in uniform, I was the gay, independent "swinging stewardess."

Anger had become my way of life, and being highly explosive I often yelled at this wonderful and patient man. "It's great sport living in sin, isn't it?" That was before living together became so popular.

Sin — what a strange little word. When I was growing up, it seemed my family had a wonderful vocabulary and always used newer and bigger words I couldn't quite keep up with. I learned a lot of swear words, too, but the only *dirty* word I ever learned was *sin*. That word was only appropriate when used to scoff at those who spoke of it seriously, whoever that was. I didn't actually know any one who did, but I grew up to hate the word and never really knew what it meant. It certainly didn't apply to me or my family or anyone I liked. I recall it had something to do with being immoral. But after all, who was immoral? It was all relative.

If anyone were to question my life-style, I could answer proudly, "You have no right to judge me, for I am not ashamed of the way I live." Why was I feeling so guilty now? I wasn't raised in a puritanical environment. Why guilt was a sign of an unbalanced philosophy! One should never be encumbered by feelings of guilt. I had always been taught to be uninhibited. What was wrong with me?

I was living a double life, and it was difficult to keep the two lives separate. My checkbook carried one name, my driver's license another. My mail carried a combination of names, and I knew my postman was the only one who knew the truth. I developed a healthy respect for the confidence a U. S. mailman carries around with him. I ached to wipe the past clean and start over again; so the first thing I did was quit the airlines and force this good man out of my life. He was an innocent by-stander in the way of an accident.

Loneliness and fear still accompanied my every waking hour and began to take over my sleep. Nightmares were constant, and guilt never left me. I seriously entertained thoughts of suicide again, planning a more thorough job — this time the girls with me. The only thing that kept me from driving all three of us over a cliff was the fear that just one of us would survive.

We moved again, and I had great hopes of making that move another new starting point. While I was only four blocks from our previous residence, I tried not to go back where neighbors knew me before.

I could not reach out to my family. I felt they all had problems enough of their own. Besides that, my phony veneer would not allow them to see the real truth about myself. I longed to seek refuge in my mother, but she was in northern California and seemed too far away. Visits with my father were too infrequent to load him up with my burdens now.

Since I could find no fox hole to crawl into, I tried to dodge familiar faces from any part of my past. I would hope not to bump into people I knew and finally got to a point where I didn't care about being with or seeing any one at any time. If I *had* to be, it was miserable the entire time. Wearing the mask of smiles became too painful, so I took refuge in my security of "nothingness." I lived each day wishing there wouldn't be another.

One day I found myself standing behind a former dinner date at the checkstand in the market. I was panicky. Before he could notice me, I quickly left my bulging grocery cart and walked to the rear of the market. Dazed with fear at having to look anyone in the face, I hid behind a canned foods display. When I thought it was safe, I sneaked out of the market without my groceries and went home to cry my heart out.

One of my more desperate prayers was, "God, if you're really there, please don't let another day happen to me."

XI

"GOD, IF YOU'RE REALLY THERE ..." I had not yet come to the place of believing he had spared my life so far. *If* you're really there? What could I know? I had never sought him to find out what he expected of me, but I expected him to appear like a huge genie whenever I called out the magic word *God*.

Days did continue to happen to me in spite of my plea. My turbulent six years of "single" life had taken its toll.

One Sunday morning our landlady and her little girl invited Lauri to go to church with them. "That sounds fine, Lauri. Go get on a dress." What a relief. I wasn't planning anything but to lie in bed all day again, and now I'd have one less kid around to bug me for something to do. Most of my time was slowly consumed by lying in bed crying with the covers over my head. Emptiness was now holding hands with guilt, and alcohol helped to ease the pain.

Lauri returned far too soon from church and ignited the fuse that caused an explosion within me. She carried with her a small brightly colored pamphlet that read, "All have sinned ..." I blew up: "For __'s sake, what the hell did they tell you all morning? Did they fill you full of this kind of crap for two hours?" I don't think anyone within two blocks of our apartment escaped the rotten venom that continued to spew from me as I tore that pamphlet to tiny bits.

When I finally simmered down, I was exhausted, so I took a drink of brandy and went back to bed for the rest of the day, stewing in my miserable thoughts. Brandy was my cure-all. I thought if I stuck to the more elegant booze, I was safe. Only alcoholics drank the cheap stuff.

Our landlords lived in front of us. I knew they were churchgoers and felt sorry for the little girl because she *had* to go to church every Sunday. Her daddy would putter around the yard whistling and singing "What a Friend We Have in Jesus." Needless to say we had little in common, other than my monthly rent check. Going to church and singing those church songs were pleasant enough, I thought, but carrying it a bit far. Now this junk they were giving my little girl . . . I promised myself to avoid them at all cost. While I wallowed in my bed of miserable seclusion, I pitied *them* because they sang Jesus songs!

Before this I had entertained the idea of the three of us getting dolled up some Sunday and going to church. Well, I decided, church will have to get along without us now. I mumbled to myself as I excused my behavior of the morning. ". . . telling my little girl about that dirty word *sin*. Surely they weren't serious?"

Two very long weeks passed, and my landlady extended the invitation to go to church again, only this time she asked all three of us. My memory of the previous Sunday was not as vivid now. Alesen wasn't particularly interested, but I thought, "Well, it's a pleasant day for a ride along the coast, and maybe I can find out what this sin business is all about."

Lauri and I dressed in our Sunday best. I deliberately chose to wear a bright, hot pink dress for shock value and unknowingly headed for an old-fashioned gospel service in Laguna Beach. Had I been aware of where we were going, I'd have gotten out and run back home, but we were already there before I realized it and it was too late. I was the one who suffered shock.

We sat in the back of the room, and I was glad in case I needed to make a hasty exit. The whole thing seemed ridiculously square as I listened to some preacher with a Southern accent. My family would die if they could see me now, I thought. I had been warned against this kind of thing since childhood.

When the preacher began to speak again, I put on my glasses to get a better look. What a cute guy, I almost said aloud, but I found myself listening to his words. For some reason I knew he *cared* about the real deep needs of people, the needs I had long ago given up on and covered over with depression. He wasn't just talking — he was reading and clearly explaining subjects from that mysterious book called the Bible.

As he continued to read, I began to suspect that my landlords had called ahead to tell him I was going to be there. He was talking about my needs, my hurts, and my feelings — yet without condemnation. His voice was filled with understanding and compassion, the combination of which stirred a different kind of hope than I had ever known before.

Then the people in that room began to pray as a group. I became fascinated. The preacher would lead the prayer aloud as everyone else bowed their heads and closed their eyes. They appeared to be serious about the whole thing. I thought I knew what prayer was — a big joke. But this was different! This preacher spoke as though some live God was standing right there listening to every word.

At the close of the service, everyone sang what I had always regarded as really dumb hymns. I was very curious to see what kind of people would come here Sunday after Sunday to read the Bible, pray such earnest prayers, and sing those silly hymns. They must just be a bunch of weirdos with nothing else going for them, I summed up.

When the service ended, I stood boldly in the back of the room to look squarely into the faces of the people leaving to find out who they were and what they looked like. I grew up with the impression that serious churchgoers were dull and out of touch with modern times. They only stood in the way of progress. I was honestly surprised to find that these were happy, bright people. The women were fashionable and attractive. The men were masculine and sharp looking. I was stunned by the genuine kindness shown to me as a visitor. These weren't kooky or illiterate people; they were bright and friendly and made me feel like a special guest. More than anything else, I remember the happiness that beamed in their faces, and I studied each one.

Then I spotted a face from my past. In that little congregation of people, I recognized someone I knew. This bothered me — I was trying to run away from my past and everything connected with it.

Nanci and I recognized each other and called each other by name instantly as if we had met just the week before. I hunted for somewhere to duck, but Nanci seemed to look right past my anxiety. She made me feel as if she truly cared that we had met once again after all these years, as if she had been waiting for this for some time.

How strange, I thought. Nanci and I had known each other briefly in the sixth grade and only because we had a mutual friend. Besides that she lived on the other side of town then and we saw each other just a few times. Why should we so easily recognize each other after twenty years? In disgust I reminded myself that I had a terrible time remembering people I had met only the previous day.

Nanci interrupted the conversation I was having with my memory to ask if I'd enjoyed the church service. I looked about me rather than at her, trying to express an air of independence and an I-could-care-less attitude. "Well," I replied, "I've found my thing in a spiritual kind of group too." I continued bravely, "It's a program call NA built on the same foundation as AA but dealing with problems of neurosis rather than alcoholism."

I told her I was a neurotic just as I had seen alcoholics in the program bravely admit they were alcoholics. I think I made an attempt to invite her to go with me sometime, but the gesture was too weak. I really wasn't concerned with whether or not I ever saw her again.

When I returned home from church, I realized I had forgotten to ask the question about sin, and it was still nagging at me. I admittedly enjoyed going to that church, but that problem of sin kept cropping up and spoiled the thought of ever going back again.

Nanci called me later on that day and suggested that we get together very soon. She sounded sincerely interested, and I detected a tone of real love in her voice. I didn't understand this at all, for I had come to believe that love was too elusive. It was something I had neither looked for or wanted from anybody again; so I asked myself, What do you 'spose she wants from you?

XII

A FEW DAYS LATER Nanci called to invite me to a home Bible study that was to be taught by the man I referred to as "the cute little preacher."

"I hope you will like the Bible study," she said as we drove together down the coast.

"I've tried everything else," I said, "guess a little Bible study won't hurt me."

Then she shared with me that she had searched in education, philosophy, psychology, and all the other modern sciences for the answers to life. She had found them at last in the Bible. I was a little bugged that she had put down philosophy as a dead end. That was *it* as far as I was concerned, and I was not about to admit my searching was in vain. But I mustered up some tolerance for her until we reached our destination.

When we arrived, I found once again a group of people who seemed so happy, loving, and friendly. Outside of that little church on Sunday I never remembered seeing a group like this anywhere else I had ever been. The "happiest" group of people I knew were found in bars around 6:00 P.M., and that was only temporary.

About fifteen people had gathered in this lovely comfortable home. Everyone was friendly and warm without being drippy and sweet and seemed to know the preacher on a first-name basis.

Nanci introduced us. "Lee, I'd like you to meet Mike Montgomery." He was a much bigger man than I thought. I looked up, we shook hands, and I felt an instant bond between us. I finally got past his good looks and remembered his words from the previous Sunday morning. Their content had found a niche in the vacant spot in my heart. I wondered if he knew that.

Mike was dressed casually in slacks and open-necked sweater. I don't know what I expected, but I was surprised that the atmosphere was congenial and comfortable. My only unrest was knowing I didn't possess whatever it was that made these other people beam, but I tried to "look" the way they did.

We settled down together in one room, and Mike began the evening by asking what had brought each of us to that study. As he started around the room, three or four other people briefly did their bit, but I didn't hear what they said. I was too busy deciding what great profound insight I could lay on this bunch to prove I had my intellect in order. Then I heard my name. ". . . And, Lee, what brings you here tonight?"

"Well," I began . . . and paused while trying to choose which attitude to adopt — pride or humility? Pride won out, and I continued in verbal grandeur: "I think the Bible is obviously just a good history book, and since history repeats itself, maybe I can learn where I fit into this particular cycle of history."

That was it: profound, honest, and certainly proud. Why wasn't everybody applauding? Why didn't the rest of the evening focus around total agreement with the point I had just made? Little did I know that I had just told Mike more about myself in that brief summary than anything else I might have said, though I had said it hoping to mask the real Lee Hayes who was lost, lonely, and sad.

When each person had taken his or her turn, Mike opened his Bible, smiled a beautiful broad smile, and softly announced: "Genesis 1:1, 'In the beginning God created the heavens and the earth.'" And everyone turned to the first book, first chapter, first verse of the Bible.

For a second I panicked as I held this very thick book on my lap. "Good grief!" I whispered. "If we're starting at the very beginning, how long are we going to be here?"

My dread melted into complete fascination as the group dissected this one verse together. Mike explained details for about an hour and a half, and I was totally enveloped in the study when it came to a close too soon. Heads bowed, and a quiet prayer of thanks was shared by all. Then friendly chatter stirred around the room. I sat still to recall some of the brand new information I had just been given. Though I didn't understand everything I heard, I was convinced that whatever else the Bible had to say must be true. I had only to look around me to see that no mere man could have put the earth and stars together.

While we sat around afterwards with coffee and donuts, I had a chance to get closer to Mike to ask what I thought would be some intelligent questions. "How do you know God *is*? It would sure help if I could see him and have some concrete evidence," I admitted, letting down my pride about half an inch.

"You can see him!" was the answer. "Jesus Christ is God in human flesh. Just take a good look at him."

If I was supposed to respond at that point, I couldn't. His answer pinned my feet to the ground and sent a steel rod up my spine. I tried to say something intelligent to close the gap of silence while Mike looked into my face, but I couldn't move. "Wow! That's strong," I said to myself. He continued to speak, but I couldn't hear his words. That last statement hit me again, returning with such force I almost lost my balance. It also irritated me that he spoke with such authority and directness. I could not grasp the idea that Jesus was God. Too much! I had to catch one of these people off guard and see if they were putting me on.

As I leaned against the wall holding one shaky cup of coffee, I remembered my early church-going experience with my Catholic friends and recalled how they would say, "God the Father, God the Son, God the Holy Ghost." So that's where that bit came from, I thought to myself, not realizing my first piece of the puzzle was being set in place.

It was some time later when I could relate to the awesome bewilderment experienced by a couple of

Christ's disciples as they asked among themselves,
"What manner of man is this that he can calm the seas
at his command?"

XIII

THE FOLLOWING SUNDAY the girls and I went back to church. This time I insisted Alesen come along.

Once again Nanci expressed a desire to get together and talk about the things that we had heard at church. What was this pulling I felt — this constant tugging to run one minute and stay the next?

As we sat in Nanci's home, she told me that Jesus Christ provided the answer to salvation for everyone, the answer for our guilt and shame, loneliness and turmoil. Now I didn't mind going to church and having a little Bible study, but preaching from her I didn't need. I didn't mind looking at Jesus from a distance, but she kept bringing him closer, and I got a little nervous.

With the same attitude of standing over a produce stand to make a selection, I admitted, "I need something, I know. All this is very fascinating, but I'm not quite sure I'm ready to accept all that stuff that goes with being a Christian." What stuff was I talking about? I didn't know what stuff a Christian was made of. A do-gooder? Yes, I thought, that's it. So forget it.

Hoping to shock Nanci a little (since that was my hobby anyway), I said, "I couldn't make it as a Christian because of some of the things I've done in my past." I wanted to scream out those crummy things that plagued me now.

Nanci wasn't going to be put off that easily. She persisted in talking about the things of Jesus Christ: his life, why he lived, why he died. But when she got on the subject of the crucifixion and resurrection, I could hardly take it. This hit a tender spot.

When I was a little girl shortly after my parents divorced, a neighbor took me to a movie at some church that showed the crucifixion of Jesus Christ. I remember running from the room crying for that wonderful man. Even at the age of nine or ten, I knew that he didn't deserve that kind of treatment because apparently he hadn't done anything wrong.

I finally asked Nanci the big question: "What about the sin business?" Her direct and simple answer surprised me.

"Sin," she said, "is the condition of every man that keeps him separated from God. It's the act of disobedience against God and doing your own thing with indifference to what God would want you to do."

Funny, I thought, I can take that. But when she started the Adam-and-Eve-with-the-fruit jazz, I began to fight intellectually (I thought). Besides that, I said to myself, what would my family think if they knew I was listening to this garbage? But she continued with the story which had never really been clear to me before. I found myself believing that she was talking about two real people who were designed *by* God, *for* God, with everything else planned for them, but who chose to use their own will and do what God had asked them *not* to do. And that's where all the trouble began.

There was a lull in the conversation, and I felt obliged to take up space with some sensational truths of my own. "Well," I began nervously, "God is a God of love! He doesn't care what we do as long as we do our best." I was torn between feeling as if I knew everything and nothing. "Doesn't he love us anyway?"

She came back with a positive yes. "But because of his love for us, he naturally cares about what we do and how we live. The choice is ours, just as it was with Adam and Eve." She went on with that same assurance Mike had: "We can acknowledge him as God or try to be little gods ourselves and run our lives the way *we* want to." She was speaking in generalities, but I was so uncomfortable because this was certainly my situation.

Her eyes grew softer, and when she made a move, I was scared to death she was going to lean over to touch me. She only spoke gently after a quiet second, "Lee, the life he offers is a full, rich, peaceful fellowship with him." That tugging returned; I wanted to run away, and I wanted to stay.

While glancing around the room, nervously crossing and uncrossing my legs, I snapped, "God doesn't look upon us as doing anything wrong!" I fought some more, but I noticed I was the only one arguing; she wasn't. I don't know where I got my information to "enlighten" her, but I knew where she was getting hers. Practically everything she told me was followed up by a verse or two out of her Bible.

"He loves us as a father," she said, "and doesn't want us to destroy our lives. He has always been willing to offer us a better way of living."

How does she know I've ruined my life? I wondered. I haven't even told her about it. When she finished, she just looked deep into my face with a new kind of love and with sparkling, peaceful eyes.

I started to shiver inside, and fearing she would notice, I thought it best to change the subject, but I found it difficult to speak. When I tried, I thought my teeth would chatter.

"Well," I said, "I've got to get some things cleaned up in my life before I can become a Christian." I crossed my legs and arms with some sort of finality as if that gesture alone might end the conversation.

Nanci's eyes were turned toward her living-room window where she stared at the ocean view that spread across the front of her house. It worked, I thought, she's all through preaching to me. But she startled me when she spoke again without turning her head.

"I used to feel just like you do, but I came to Christ just as I was and then he began to straighten out my life *for* me." Turning toward me again with a soft and gentle smile, "He'll do the same for you."

I don't want all this, I screamed to myself inside. What am I doing here? But I was glued to the chair, wishing I could keep my mouth shut and hang on to what she had just said. I visualized Alesen and Lauri running home after falling in a mud puddle. Would I close the door on them, or help them out of their dirty clothes and bathe them?

Nanci still hadn't said anything to offend me, yet I went home very disturbed. She had given me some things to read, and as I read I ached to have what Nanci had. She displayed a peace and security that I could not understand. Her life wasn't a bed of roses; I could see that. But she wasn't bothered by her problems. She took each day as it came along.

My philosophy of living a "day at a time" simply meant getting along the best I could without getting into too much trouble and hurting as few people as possible. But it wasn't working. When I dared to be honest and face myself with the facts, I knew I *was* hurting myself and other people too.

That night I lay in bed with a little book called the New Testament, whatever that was, and I read some strange words. They said things I had never heard before. I knew *about* Jesus Christ and had decided he was a great teacher, a good philosopher, and a great prophet. However, I didn't actually know what he really taught or prophesied.

Alesen and Lauri asked me once what a Christian was. I stopped and thought. "I guess a Christian is a person who tries to follow the teachings of a great teacher called Jesus Christ."

"Are we Christians?" they asked.

"Sure!" I answered very proudly and dropped it, mainly because I didn't know what else to say.

I continued to read the words that Jesus spoke as recorded in this little Book. "I am the way, the truth, and the life," he said. "No man can come to the Father but by me." Whew! What did that mean? "He that hates me hates my Father also." Why would he say a thing like that? I didn't have a reason to hate him. "This is the work of God that you believe on him whom he has sent."

I could hardly sleep that night as my mind raced through questions about God that kept cropping up. I had never had such a pulling and gnawing concern about spiritual matters before. I seemed to be plagued with all the things Nanci told me. I had to talk to her again.

Struggling with my new hunger pains for truth, I recalled how I was the one who held the beautiful deep thoughts and philosophies. I didn't need any more. My innate goodness and intelligence would one day be unleashed once I found that man in my life to love and understand me. Deep spiritual thoughts should belong only to the pope. I tried to brush them aside.

XIV

WHEN NANCI INVITED US over again after church on Mother's Day, I was pleased. The service was very moving as Mike shared out of the Bible God's view of what a mother was designed to be. I couldn't believe my ears. At last, I thought, direction, help, concern, and hope for me to be the kind of mother I always yearned to be. If God had a blueprint, I was going to get a copy as soon as possible. I needed so much to have some insight on what to tell my daughters about themselves, other people, life, sex, their expectations and disappointments, and most of all how to love. I had none of these answers myself.

I was eager now to have Nanci "preach" to me. We sat in her living room again while her two girls and Alesen and Lauri swam outside in her pool. She read John 3:16: "For God so loved the world, that he gave his only begotten Son, that whosoever believeth in him should not perish, but have everlasting life."

"Well," I asked defensively, "what does that mean, 'everlasting life'?"

She said, "Exactly what it says," and continued: "There *is* a heaven. It lasts for eternity, and God wants you to be there with him. It's your choice to make."

"Well, isn't everybody going to be there?" I asked indignantly.

Nanci replied humbly, "God offered his Son, Jesus, to provide the way to heaven. Jesus himself said, 'I am the way, the truth and the life, no man comes to the Father but by me.'" She quoted the verse I remembered reading myself.

This was hard to take, but I was touched by the strength in those words. Were they true or not? I had to find out because suddenly I knew that if they were not true, that made Jesus a liar and put him on a bar stool right next to a half-dozen other men I had walked away from in the last few years. I didn't want to do that to Jesus.

I was still not offended, for it wasn't Nanci speaking. It was her voice, yes, but every word in answer to my questions was coming out of the Bible. Then she had me read Revelation 3:20: "Behold, I stand at the door, and knock; if any man hear my voice, and open the door, I will come in to him and will dwell with him and he with me." These were the words of Christ. He was asking if he could come into my life, my heart, and live his life through me. If I let him, I could not only know peace on this earth but peace throughout eternity — in heaven.

Now the other pieces of the "Big Three" began to fit: God the Father (Creator), God the Son (Jesus), God the Holy Spirit (his life in me). With some difficulty, I finally admitted to Nanci, "I'm not really too concerned about eternity, but I sure need some peace here on earth." With this confession I found a comfort, at last, just to be with Nanci. She was real, and I believed I could trust her. She really cared for me in spite of my efforts to be cold and aloof.

At this point it was very clear to me that Christ was the only man who ever promised such a gift as peace, and now I wanted to know how to get it.

"Believe on the Lord, Jesus Christ, and thou shall be saved" was the verse she pointed out for me to read aloud.

Oh, no! Memories of my youth flashed through my mind. "Jesus Saves" read a huge sign on the cross of a funny old church up the street from our house. We kids used to fool around at nights, and for lack of something else to do we'd go up to that church and watch what went on inside through the wide open doors. It's stupid, we thought. Any church that's open during the week is weird!

One warm summer night the tall thin preacher spotted three of us standing outside and asked if we wanted to come forward to be saved. We giggled, made a lunge through the door, then "chickened-out" and ran home, laughing at the thought that we needed to be saved. Saved from what? We mocked the preacher's words back and forth at each other; it seemed so dumb, and my brothers and sister backed me up as I shared my adventure with them.

Nanci drew me back to the present by asking if I'd like her to pray with me and invite Jesus Christ into my life. She startled me but had answered my yet unasked question, How do I do it?

The idea of prayer was no longer a stranger to me; I had shared it each Sunday in church for the past three weeks. However, I wasn't sure I could pray out loud. The struggle that tore me apart during every other conversation was no longer with me. Nevertheless, I found myself pleading with my heart and eyes, "Yes, please do help me to pray."

All of my life it seemed I had tried to fit into a mold that I thought would suit and please my family. I surely didn't have the intellect and artistic ability of my oldest brother, the wit and charm of my sister, nor the sense of humor and musical talent of my other brother. I knew my mother loved me anyway, but wasn't too sure about my father since our times together were so few. "If only I could make my family proud of me . . ." was my biggest dream. That would be the height of success, or so I thought.

I had never realized that this feeling of inferiority and vacuum in my life could only be filled with God, and I felt a miserable failure in my families' eyes if I didn't capture their attention at every opportunity.

Now for the first time in my life I left my family far behind. I turned and didn't even consider what they would do, think, say, or feel. The decision I was about to make was without any excuse or explanation to anyone but God. This was between him and me.

My years of loneliness had never been inviting. My flexible morals were not valuable enough to pass on to Alesen and Lauri. Vanity had not kept me youthful, and I did not have a single dependable friend. The weight of resentment for my fellow man was a very heavy load, and I couldn't hang on to these things any longer.

With my first honest feelings of humility and without any prompting from Nanci, I felt my spirit surrender, and I slid off the couch and onto my knees at her coffee table. Nanci joined me, and we closed our eyes. She began: "Our most precious Heavenly Father, here is one who wants the peace only you can offer. You said that where two or more are gathered together in your name, you are there too. She *wants* to pray. In Jesus' name, please help her."

There was a quiet pause, and I knew that God was waiting for me. It was in Nanci's living room, not a church building, that I came face to face with the God who made heaven and earth, the resurrected Christ who lived to meet me where I was. My eyes were closed, but I knew he was present in that room, and out of the depths of my being came words I had never uttered before. I asked Jesus Christ to come into my heart and life and help me out of the mess I had gotten into.

I was not yet finished praying when I was suddenly made fully aware of what sin really was and admitted that I, too, was a sinner. My life was proof of my indifference to God. Remembering the words Nanci read to me that God forgives our sins when we ask forgiveness and that Christ suffered on the cross to erase my sins, I asked for that forgiveness for the first time in my life.

I had spent many years trying to cover up my ugly past and making excuses for my mistakes. But I found myself spreading them out wide open on a table before a real God and seeing them with his eyes. I now knew what confession was: agreeing with God and seeing transgression as he sees it. And when he, my Maker, forgave me, the burden was lifted.

A sense of warm relief began to flow through me even before I finished my prayer. When I opened my eyes, they were blurred with tears of joy. I had a new Spirit within me. I didn't want to leave that peaceful moment. But I had stayed as long as was necessary and ended with thanks to God for what he had just given me. "So this was receiving Christ as your personal Savior," I reflected. "He cares about us individually! That's reassuring. He wants us to know him in a personal way, and the problem that keeps us apart is simply sin in our lives and not being willing to admit it. That was certainly true in my case." The tears smeared my grinning face.

I had tried to be a self-made individual. I had only to look back over my recent past to see what I had made of myself. I wasn't very well constructed; I hadn't done a good job. It was so clear and simple now.

Nanci asked me where Christ was at that moment. "Inside me," I answered joyfully. "I feel life — a new start on life," though I knew I did not have to tell her what I felt. She knew! That peace and that clean feeling I had been looking for for years was finally mine.

"Jesus," I reflected, "So this was that powerful man who said, 'Let him who is without sin cast the first stone.', as He stood to protect a woman caught in the act of adultery while her accusers yelled and screamed in self-righteous condemnation? . . . So this was the man who had the authority to say to that woman, 'Your sins are forgiven. Go and sin no more'."

I was a baby Christian, but God didn't waste any time waiting for me to grow up before he began to reveal to me his miraculous ways. As Nanci and I sat in her living room, she confessed that for the past two years my name (as she had known it twenty years earlier) frequently popped into her mind. I was astounded, for I had also been remembering her during the same period of time.

We rejoiced together that without any doubt God had been preparing us both for this glorious experience together. For the second time in my life, I gave thanks to God. I searched for peace apart from God and found confusion. I looked for love apart from God and was hurt. I longed for rest apart from God and became weary. I wanted forgiveness apart from God and ended up condemned in my guilt. I sought God apart from Jesus Christ and was lost.

I suppose God could have arranged it another way, another time, and with a different person, but he knew my needs. I needed a friend, and now with Jesus as our common bond, he knew Nanci was just the right one for me. We have experienced six years of joy, sorrow, tears, belly laughs, and thanksgiving in the

113

love of our wonderful God who brought us together. And we giggle with the excitement of two little girls when we remember that we get to share and enjoy life for all eternity.

The entire mystery of life continued to unfold during the next few weeks. I experienced the beginning of a personal relationship with a living God, a loving Father, the Creator of life, the One who holds the universe in perfect balance.

I began to see that all my self-improvement courses, my frivolous relationships, and my discontent as a parent were the result of not turning to the only one who knew the answers. When I did, I realized that I did not merely *have* problems, I was *the* problem, and Christ was the solution.

At last! Something to give my children. No longer was I baffled about what to tell them of life. No longer did I weep and shiver at the thought that they would have to grow up to fend for themselves, only to retreat to empty bitterness. I looked at them and thanked God that he hadn't allowed me to drive off a cliff as I had contemplated.

God immediately began to heal some gaping wounds in my heart and started to build a family out of the three of us. He gave me no hint that he would change our circumstances, but he promised to change us in spite of the circumstances.

I had no more insight into Phil's disappearance than I had before, but I had new peace about him.

Bitterness and fear left me. God assured me that he knew the situation, too, and gave me a new awareness: If Phil was to be a part of us, he would live in the good memories I could now share with the girls about the kind of human being their father once was, the kind of man he was when we were married, and the way he loved them when they were so little. I have not known a nightmare since Mother's Day, 1969.

At last I could admit my imperfections to Lauri and Alesen. I told them I was going to have to put all my trust in Jesus to help me. The three of us were swept up in the arms of fellow Christians who had also discovered a personal relationship with Christ. It was exciting to hear them share their new births into the family of God.

I was eager to share my experience — especially with my family. My sister had moved into her beach house down the coast; so one beautiful Sunday after church I drove down to visit her. She was with my brother in the back yard when I drove up. They knew I had been going to church lately and remarked how I had apparently gotten "hooked" on it. I found myself defensive because church had come to mean so much.

I wanted to run to the car for my brand-new Bible and reveal to them the wonderful truths I had learned, but I knew I couldn't remember where to find all those good things. I'll go get my Bible anyway, I thought, and maybe the Lord would just let the Book fall open to where all those life-changing verses are written. But God knew what he was doing. That was too much meat for a toothless, brand-new baby.

All my life I had longed to be able to offer something of value to my family. All my other quests were shallow and meaningless. Now that I finally had something of substance to share with them, I could only admit that I knew Christ was the answer to my life's emptiness.

XV

ONE RICH FULL WEEK had passed when the girls and I were invited to a mother-daughter conference at a place called Forest Home in the San Bernardino Mountains. We were told only that we'd have a beautiful weekend and share a cabin with Nanci and her two girls.

The night before we left, Alesen called me into her room to tuck her in bed. I guessed that Nanci's daughters had gotten her excited about the forthcoming trip from their standpoint, and I thought she wanted to talk about it.

Alesen knew she had a new mother, one who had a long way to go but who finally had a taste of happiness. This adorable little girl had carried a heavy burden for her young years while she watched me tear to pieces the security that rightfully belonged to her and her sister. I was so sorry for the damage I had done, but now I could trust Jesus Christ to mend the wounds.

The bright moonlight streamed through Alesen's bedroom window as I sat down on her bed.

"Mom, I want to become a Christian, too. I asked Christ to come into my heart a couple of days ago, but I want to make sure. How can I know?" she asked.

I quoted the verse in which Jesus said he would come in to anyone who opened the door, that he would stay there and never ever leave. "Do you believe that, Alesen?"

"Yes," she said, and asked if she could pray with me. We bowed our heads in the still of her room as she confirmed her faith in Jesus Christ, and he was there with us. I had just shared with my daughter the greatest gift of truth there is: the love of God the Father, Son, and Holy Spirit, who at that moment became the Comforter, Teacher, and Keeper of her life.

Lauri also discovered her need for Jesus. Earlier that same day she was in the kitchen and suddenly became convinced of her sin (remembering the recent difficulty she was having with taking things from her classroom that didn't belong to her), and she began to cry. So from all she had heard at Sunday school and in conversation with other children and adults, she asked Jesus to forgive her and come into her heart. She said those tears turned from sadness to happiness as she knew his forgiveness and she became a Christian there in the kitchen — eight years old.

Because my brand-new life was so rich and exciting, I just wasn't all too concerned about heaven. I figured that wherever and whatever it was would be fine with me. But when we arrived at Forest Home, I asked Nanci, "Is this heaven?"

118

"No," she laughed, "but we're one mile closer."

"Well, if heaven is anything like this," I told her, "I'm ready to go any time."

We were surrounded with brilliant green pine trees under clear blue skies during the day, and covered with warm, star-studded, pine-scented nights. Even more, Forest Home was a moment-by-moment revelation that Christ was alive, not only in my life, but in many others. I met people there whose lives had been miraculously salvaged at some valuable point in time.

I heard first-hand testimonies from the beaming faces of women who met Christ on a one-to-one basis. They, too, had discovered purpose and direction for their lives as women, wives, parents, lovers, homemakers, and neighbors. Now they continued a life of total liberation — turning it all over to the only one who can take it, the God of our universe.

At Forest Home we sang, prayed, ate, laughed, hiked, and made new discoveries of life-giving truths in the Bible, and wept when it was time to leave. I also began a deep and abiding friendship with the Apostle Paul. I could relate to his conversion as I discovered how he, too, sorrowed for having lived so long without recognizing Jesus as God's plan for life.

The questions I had asked in my youth and that had nagged at me throughout my life were finally answered; and the solutions were simple and uncomplicated — just as I had expected them to be as a child. I finally know what my relationship is to nature, now that I know my relationship to God.

My Heavenly Father had already moved me into a position to get a better look at life from his vantage point, and I could see things from his side of the fence. I was not shocked at what I saw, but surprisingly shocked at my reaction. *Playboy* magazine held nothing of interest any more. There isn't any verse in the Bible that says, "Thou shalt not read *Playboy* magazine," but my taste-buds were changed. Was God going to make me a snob? Not at all. He just let me see the futility of life where he is not the master.

The "free sex" philosophy was finally illuminated as a real blind alley. The shocking profound words of Lenny Bruce were dull compared to those of my new Jewish leader, Jesus Christ. I found that I could even thank God for all the disappointments I had experienced in the past because I could see that what he was after was me.

Now that I turned my mistakes over to God, I had to learn to trust him to handle my future. If he could do this, then he could no doubt help me in rearing the children he gave me. Depending on him for this was the first and easiest step I took as a baby Christian, and certainly the wisest thing I could do as a parent.

In those early days of newly found faith, I erroneously concluded that Christians should be perfect and never have difficulties in life. The wife of a very famous author set me straight when she said, "Christians are just as crumby as anybody else. The only difference is, they admit it . . . or should."

I know Jesus himself suffered great temptations and trials, yet he never gave in to anger, deceit, or frustration. I learned that my need for him would be a moment-by-moment dependence upon his comforting strength. But as a babe, I sometimes did not allow God to handle certain aspects of my life. I made all the mistakes new Christians usually make, and it wasn't too long before I started to order God around. I behaved like a child who asks her daddy to fix a doll and then stands in the workshop to tell him what to do.

My feminine sensitivities were heightened when I was given a new capacity to love others and a desire to submit to love. So I prayed for a chance to share that experience with a specific man. Naturally, I thought this request would be granted right away — it seemed so perfect to me.

I had been told by some of my new friends that if I prayed in specifics, God would answer me in specifics. Well, he did. The answer was a specific no!

"Hey . . ." I argued, "all your answers to prayer are supposed to be yes. How can you deny me such a neat thing?"

My dating experiences were full of concern, "Is this the one you've picked out for me, Lord?" In trying to preempt his answers I was made vulnerable to some real disappointments. "Is this the man you have chosen to be father to my children?"

"No, not this one — or that one . . . at least not for now. I shall be a Father to the fatherless."

I was soon to learn that his greatest desire for me was to be reshaped for a more effective purpose than that of wife to a step-father for Alesen and Lauri.

Obviously because I lacked the foresight he had, I suffered great moments of anxiety while I learned that his *love* and *grace* were sufficient for *all* my needs. It's my *wants* that still continue to get me in trouble. My needs are well attended to.

Because of God's ever-present love for me, I discovered my earthly family afresh. He doesn't make any mistakes when he assigns parents and other members to a family. At long last I am assured of a special love from both my father and mother, and God surely knew my need there.

I have the relationship with my dad that I yearned for as a child. It continues to be fulfilled by frequent visits over leisurely and elaborate meals, walks on the beach together, and priceless gifts he has bestowed on me such as beautiful pastel portraits he did of his granddaughters.

My mother calls herself the first Hippie, " . . . Only a happy hippy," she says, " 'cuz I never had to do the drug scene in order to love people." But to all her grandchildren, she's Walt Disney's live cartoon version of Cinderella's Fairy Godmother. What a terrific combination.

Jesus Christ gently persuaded me to let him be the head of our house and promised to teach me how to show love and administer discipline to my children.

Each day I search the Scripture to learn what he says about the parent-child relationship. Every time I complain about the girls, his response is, "Yes, I know about them. What about you?" Daily I beg him to replace my impatient spirit with his Spirit, and he is faithful to do just that. The Christian walk isn't difficult; it's just impossible without Christ.

Our Christian life does not depend on a church membership, but the girls and I have enjoyed fellowship and spiritual growth in several outstanding Bible-teaching churches. At present, we are reaping the harvest with a nondenominational group of believers in Newport Beach. We knew many of these Christians at the beginning of our spiritual walk, and they have a special place in my heart.

I am no longer alone or afraid. Alesen and Lauri have a relationship with the Father, who has provided a real home for them. We share a life in which Christ is the hub of all our activities. Together we have experienced the humility of seeking God's help whether we are at the beach on a gorgeous sunny day or in the midst of a gloomy family conflict. What a contrast to the times when God was the last one I'd call on for help and the first one I'd blame for my troubles!

Growing up is not any easier for me than it is for Alesen and Lauri. We have tripped and stumbled together in our Christian experience, but we have the freedom to enter the castle of prayer to talk boldy to the king. And he straightens out *every* situation. Why? Because the king is our Father.

In 1970 the State of California declared me a legal widow, but the year before that I was united with one who promised, "I will never leave you or forsake you." As a legal widow I am able to receive certain benefits which relieve me of the need to be employed full time. Happily, I am able to spend two and one-half days a week working in a beautiful botanical garden near the ocean in Corona del Mar. There I am free to exercise the love for growing things that was handed to me naturally from my mother and father.

Having put aside the world's psychology books, I continue to learn how to be the kind of person God wants me to be while my daughters enter womanhood as responsible young adults. Jesus Christ motivates me to share my life and join the many thousands of ancient and modern men and women who finally discovered something worthwhile to pass on to their fellow man: the never ending love of Jesus Christ.

Now I sing out with Paul: ". . . as much as is in me, I am ready to tell the Good News to you. . . . For I am not ashamed of the gospel of Christ. For it is the power of God unto salvation to everyone that believes."

Thank you, Lord, for replacing my shame with your love.